SIMPLIFIED
CHINESE
CHARACT
简体
D0827296

PENG'S CHINESE TREASURY

Simplified Chinese Characters

concept and cartoons
by
Tan Huay Peng

HEIAN

FIRST AMERICAN EDITION – 1987
Third Printing 1996

HEIAN INTERNATIONAL, INC.
1815 West 205th Street, Suite 301
Torrance, CA 90501

First published in Singapore by
Times Books International
an imprint of Times Editions Pte Ltd
Times Centre
1 New Industrial Road
Singapore 536196

ISBN 0-89346-293-4

Printed in Singapore

CONTENTS

SIMPLIFIED CHINESE CHARACTERS

Contrary to popular belief, simplified characters are not a recent innovation. In the evolution of the Chinese script, the simplification of characters has been a continual process – from the original shell and bone characters up to the modern simplified form. Not only have the number of strokes been reduced, but on the whole highly complicated characters have been made easier to write.

Shell and Bone Characters

The earliest extant writings are the **Shell and Bone** inscriptions used mainly for oracles. Such characters were engraved with a stylus on tortoise-shell and animal bone, also on bronzes and stone. These range from the complex to the relatively simple. But the lack of standardization resulted in many diversified and variant forms.

Seal Styles

The seal form was widely used for official and private seals. At this stage, simplification was already under way. In the **Great Seal Style**, for example, the character for 'assemble together' (集) was a complex ideograph indicating three short-tailed birds perched together on a tree. This was simplified to one bird on a tree – the only prevalent form in the **Small Seal Style** of that time.

Simplified Styles

The change from one style to another was largely determined by the adoption of new writing materials. The introduction of the writing brush led to the square or **Official Style** of the scribes and eventually the regular **Clerical Style**. Other even more simple styles appeared – the cursive '**Running Hand**' and the '**Grass style**' characters, described as such when people wrote quickly and with flourish without caring too much about regularity. Such styles tended to vary widely with individual writers.

Modern Simplification Process

Simplified characters came into usage as far back as 2,000 years ago. There is one difference, however, between past and present moves toward simplification. In the past, simple forms crept in without formal recognition; today simplification is a systematic and concerted process based on a set of guiding principles.

Simplification of Chinese Characters

This table depicts the gradual evolution of Chinese writing from its ancient to the present simplified form.

WHY SIMPLIFY?

To Make Writing Simpler and Faster

Most existing Chinese characters look 'architecturally' cumbersome, and are made up of a number of components; from these many can be isolated as characters in their own right. Simplification would mean reducing the number of strokes by half or one-third in some instances. We supply a few examples, and the differences are obvious.

To Aid Learning Effectively

Chinese is a script that relies heavily on memory – the more complicated the strokes the more difficult it is to remember, and efforts at learning can be greatly hindered. With simplification this no longer proves a handicap, and as a result more and more people can benefit from written Chinese.

To Make Knowledge Accessible

Simplification of characters is a welcome development in the light of today's high-technology era and expanding frontiers of knowledge, where rapid retrieval and dissemination of information has become vital. The saving on time and energy is certainly significant.

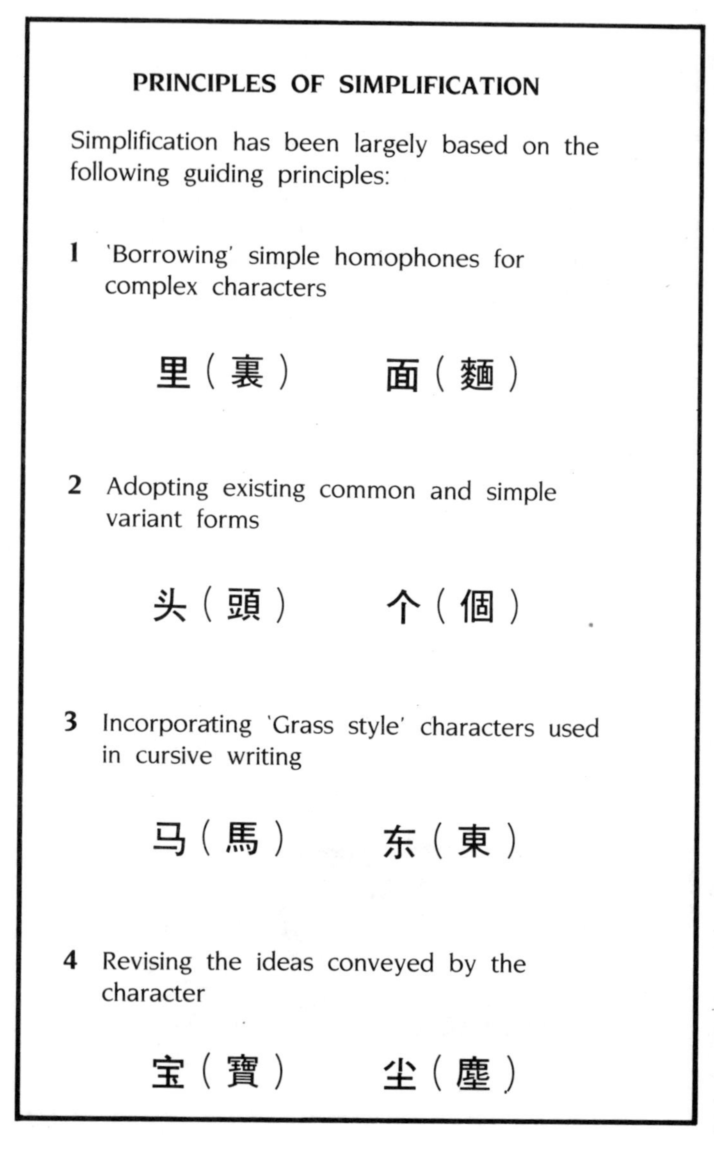

PRINCIPLES OF SIMPLIFICATION

Simplification has been largely based on the following guiding principles:

1 'Borrowing' simple homophones for complex characters

里（裏）　面（麵）

2 Adopting existing common and simple variant forms

头（頭）　个（個）

3 Incorporating 'Grass style' characters used in cursive writing

马（馬）　东（東）

4 Revising the ideas conveyed by the character

宝（寶）　尘（塵）

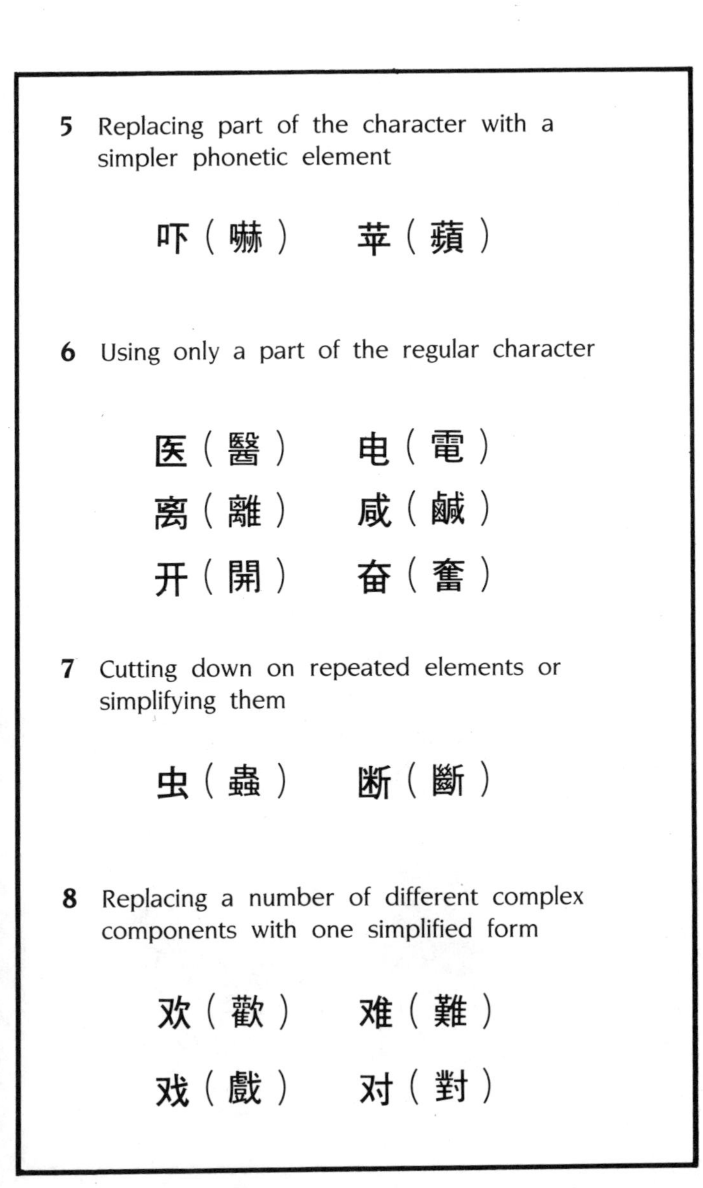

5 Replacing part of the character with a simpler phonetic element

吓（嚇）　苹（蘋）

6 Using only a part of the regular character

医（醫）　电（電）

离（離）　咸（鹹）

开（開）　奋（奮）

7 Cutting down on repeated elements or simplifying them

虫（蟲）　断（斷）

8 Replacing a number of different complex components with one simplified form

欢（歡）　难（難）

戏（戲）　对（對）

1 'Borrowing' a simpler character (which already has a meaning of its own) with the same sound, though the tone may vary. This is bound to be confusing, so if in doubt always refer to the context.

For example, 象 (elephant) is now also the simplified character for 像 (shape; resemble). Similarly, 面 (face, surface) is the simplified character for 麵 (noodles, flour).

Examples

Meaning: inside 裏 → 里 lǐ

里, also pronounced lǐ, is the character for 'mile'.

Meaning: after 後 → 后 hòu

后, also pronounced hòu, is the character for 'queen'.

Meaning: grain 穀 → 谷 gǔ

谷, also pronounced gǔ, is the character for 'valley'.

Meaning: conflict 鬥 → 斗 dòu

斗, pronounced dǒu, is the character for 'measure of 10 pint'.

Meaning: dry 乾 → 干 gān

Meaning: do 幹 → 干 gàn

干, pronounced gān, is the character for 'interfere'.

Meaning: draw, plan 劃 → 划 huà

划, pronounced huá, is the character for 'paddle'.

Meaning: roll up 捲 → 卷 juǎn

卷, pronounced juàn, is the character for 'book'.

Meaning: prepare 準 → 准 zhǔn
准, also pronounced zhǔn, is the character for 'allow'.

Meaning:
pertaining to the house 傢 → 家 jiā
家, also pronounced jiā, is the character for 'family' or 'home'.

Meaning: fasten 繫 → 系 xì
系, also pronounced xì, is the character for 'connection'.

Meaning: loose 鬆 → 松 sōng
松, also pronounced sōng, is the character for 'pine'.

Meaning: powerful 衝 → 冲 chòng
冲, pronounced chōng, is the character for 'flush'.

Meaning: beard 鬍 → 胡 hú
胡, also pronounced hú, is the character for 'careless' or 'wild'.

Meaning: hair 髮 → 发 fā

发, pronounced fā, is the character for 'distribute'.

Meaning: excuse 藉 → 借 jiè

借, also pronounced jiè, is the character for 'borrow'.

2 Opting for the simpler form (when there are 2 or more ways of writing one character). Many of these have entered common usage, especially in letter-writing or casual correspondence. It would come as no surprise to find that most people have been using these simplified forms for as long as they can remember! The only difference being that whereas previously it was a matter of style or preference, all of these have now been accepted as the standard simplified forms.

Examples

個 → 个
萬 → 万
頭 → 头
牀 → 床
卻 → 却
閒 → 閑 → 闲
兇 → 凶
祗 → 只
甚 → 什
瞭 → 了
直 → 直
腳 → 脚
羣 → 群
纔 → 才

3 Incorporating 'Grass style' characters, a style of writing rapidly and in a cursive hand, eliminating total number of strokes.

Examples

馬 → 马
魚 → 鱼
鳥 → 鸟
東 → 东
樂 → 乐
興 → 兴
亞 → 亚
車 → 车
長 → 长
寫 → 写
門 → 门
區 → 区
罔 → 冈
風 → 风

4 Ideas behind the characters are revised, pruned down to the most basic and obvious. It would be easy to figure out the meaning with a mere glance at the character.

Example: the character 滅 (extinguish) is simplified to 灭 . The most basic idea is retained – that a fire has to be snuffed out, represented by the horizontal stroke placed above the 'fire' character.

Examples

寶 → 宝
雙 → 双
陰 → 阴
陽 → 阳
塵 → 尘
筆 → 笔
義 → 义
從 → 从
國 → 国

夢 → 梦
聽 → 听
傷 → 伤
衆 → 众
櫃 → 柜
歲 → 岁
孫 → 孙
愛 → 爱
畫 → 画

PRECIOUS The regular character revealed the items considered precious to man. Under the roof (宀) he kept jade (王), porcelain (缶) and cowrie shells (貝) used as money. The simplified form shows gem or jade (玉) under the roof (宀).

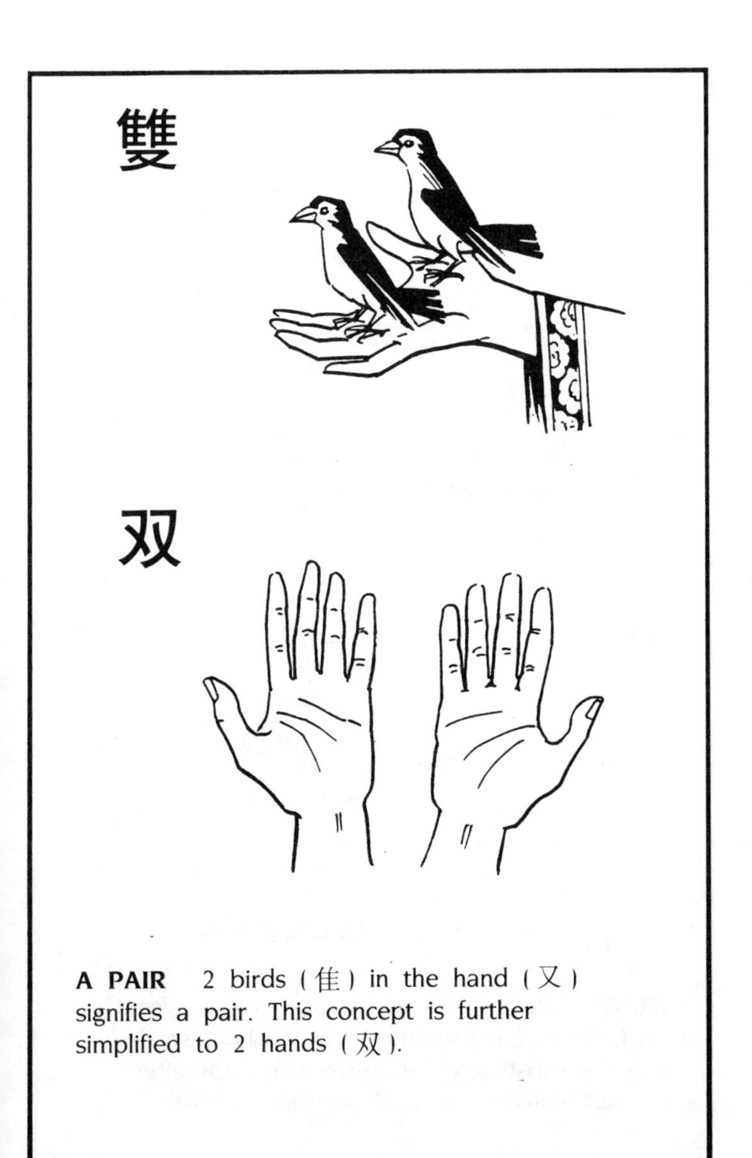

A PAIR 2 birds (隹) in the hand (又) signifies a pair. This concept is further simplified to 2 hands (双).

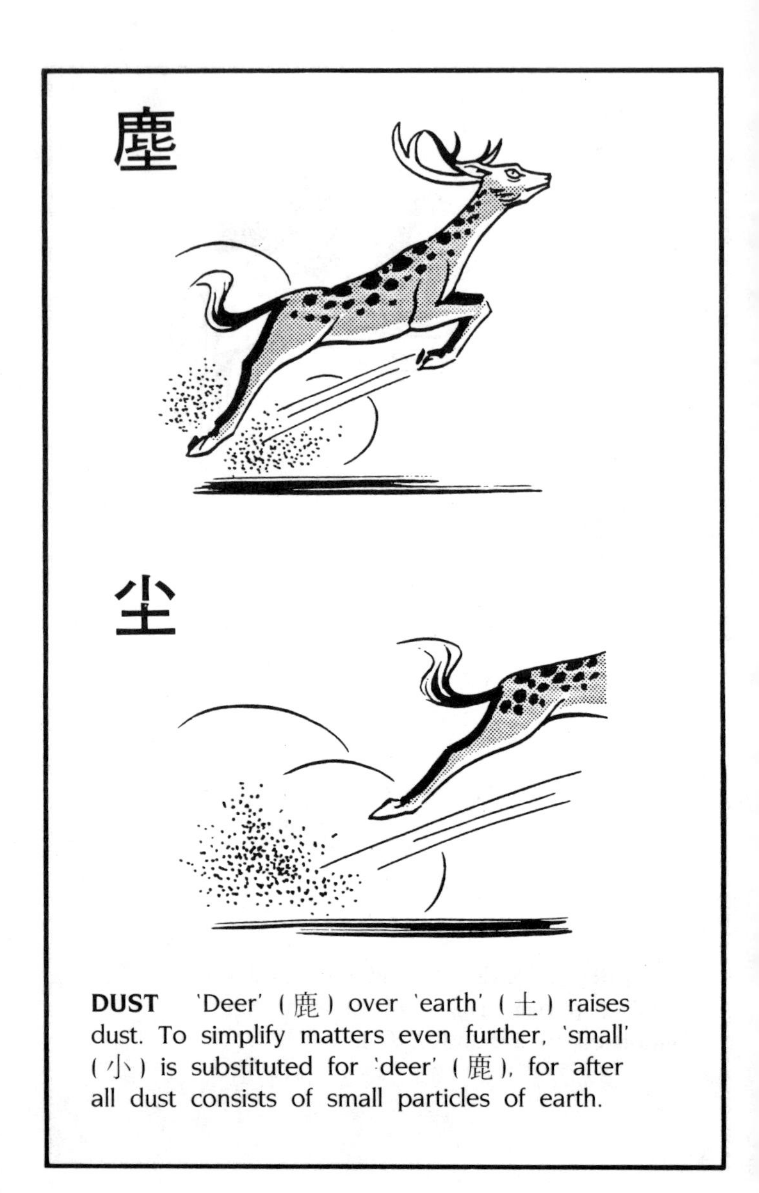

DUST 'Deer' (鹿) over 'earth' (土) raises dust. To simplify matters even further, 'small' (小) is substituted for 'deer' (鹿), for after all dust consists of small particles of earth.

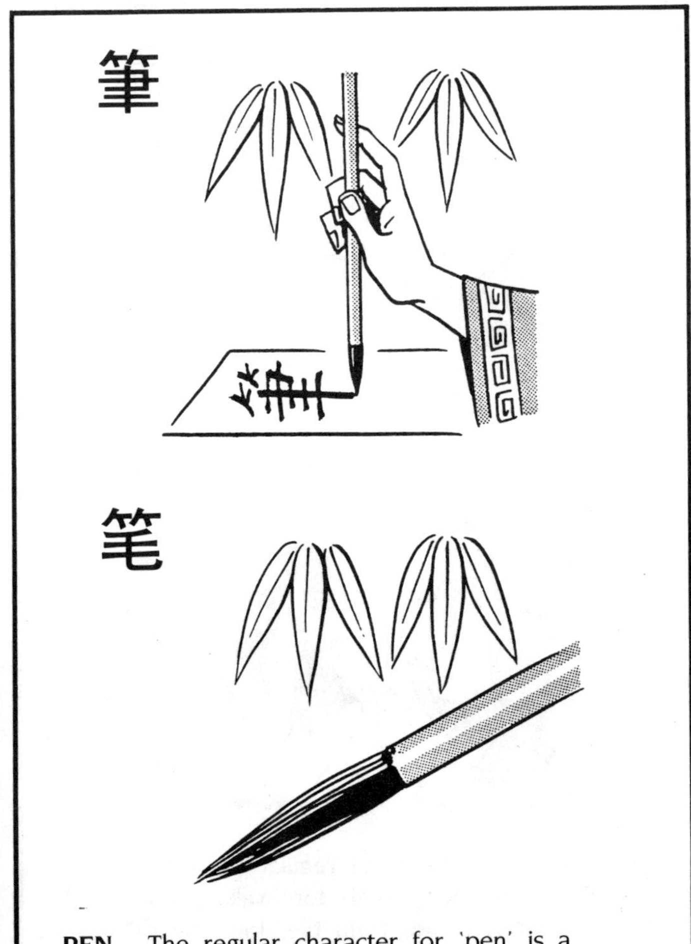

PEN The regular character for 'pen' is a composite of 2 radicals, 'bamboo' (⺮) and 'brush' (聿). The simplified form retains the 'bamboo' radical but combines it instead with 'hair' (毛).

FOLLOW Making up the regular character for 'follow' are the radicals for 'walk' (彳) and 龰 which comes from the 'foot' radical (足), as well as the 'man' radical (人). Revised and simplified, the character shows only two persons, one behind the other (从).

COUNTRY Originally, the character for 'country' combined the 'mouth' radical (口), signifying the population, and the 'weapon' radical (戈), signifying defence, within a boundary (囗). These ideas are pruned to the simplest by putting only jade (玉) inside the boundary, which symbolises the emperor, head of the country.

LISTEN The ear (耳), the eye (罒) and the heart (心) contribute to the act of listening in the regular form. The simplified character leaves us with the 'mouth' radical (口) and the 'axe' radical (斤) – to suggest, then, that what is spoken should be paid attention to!

GRANDCHILD In the regular form, the right-hand component is 系, meaning 'connection', 'system' or 'series', evidently referring here to a succession of children. To take its place in the simplified form is the component 小, bringing together the ideas of 'child' (子) and 'small' (小).

5 Replacing only part of the character with a simpler phonetic element. (Tone may however vary, as can be seen from the examples shown.) Many simplified characters fall into this category. It may be interesting to note that while many of the phonetic elements in the following examples happen to be independent characters, a general rule cannot be made. For example, 夬 is not, but one knows that 块(塊) is pronounced kuài based on our knowledge of the character 快 (fast).

Examples

xià	嚇 → 吓
yóu	郵 → 邮
gōu	溝 → 沟
chí	遲 → 迟
	(尺 is pronounced chǐ)
píng	蘋 → 苹
tài	態 → 态
fū	膚 → 肤
xiā	蝦 → 虾
	(下 is pronounced xià)

zhòng 種 → 种
(中 is pronounced zhōng)

shèng 勝 → 胜
(生 is pronounced shēng)

yōng 傭 → 佣
(用 is pronounced yòng)

jù 據 → 据
(居 is pronounced jū)

jù 懼 → 惧

lì 歷 → 历

kuài 塊 → 块

dá 達 → 达
(大 is pronounced dà)

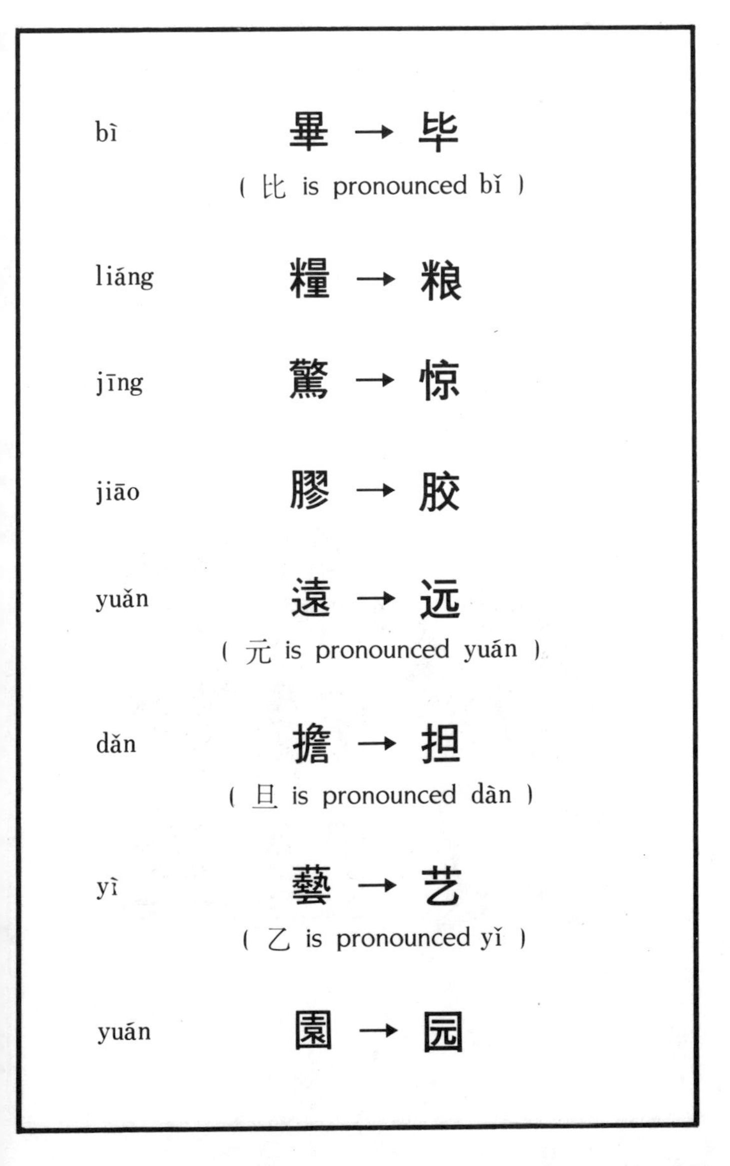

bì 畢 → 毕

(比 is pronounced bǐ)

liáng 糧 → 粮

jīng 驚 → 惊

jiāo 膠 → 胶

yuǎn 遠 → 远

(元 is pronounced yuán)

dǎn 擔 → 担

(旦 is pronounced dān)

yì 藝 → 艺

(乙 is pronounced yǐ)

yuán 園 → 园

6 Using only a part of the regular character, and this may be from top or bottom, left, right, middle, or top *and* bottom.

Examples

From the top:

醫 → 医
廣 → 广
氣 → 气
飛 → 飞
聲 → 声
築 → 筑
塗 → 涂
製 → 制
麗 → 丽

From the bottom:

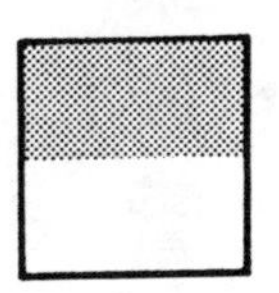

電 → 电
雲 → 云
麼 → 么

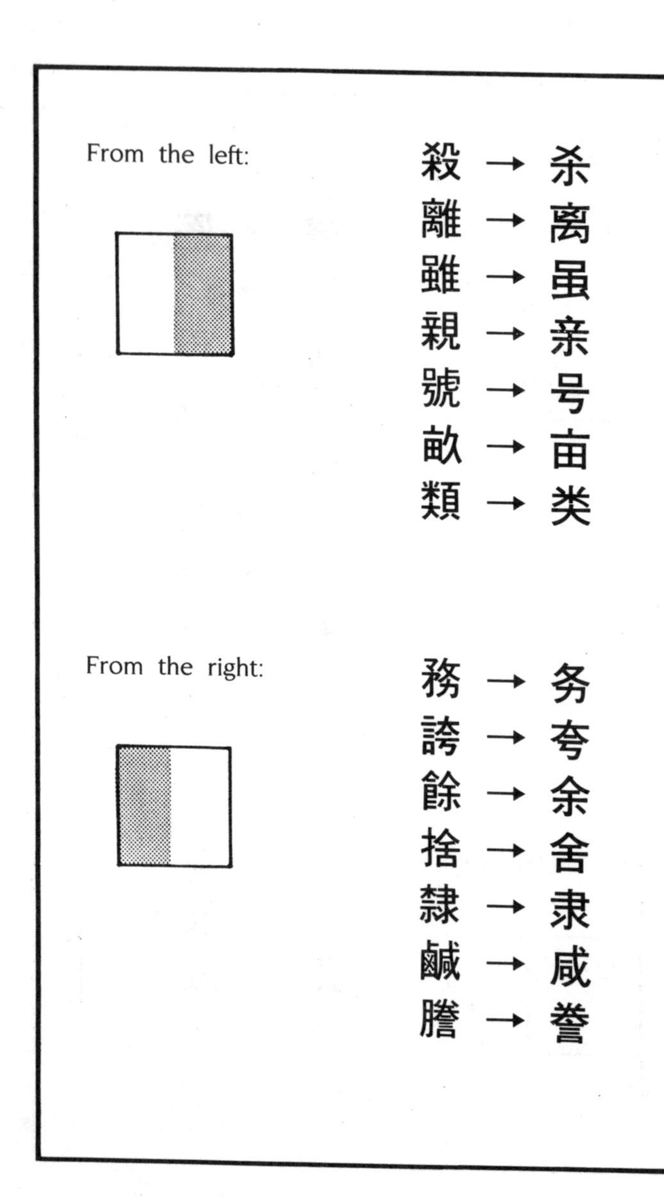
From the left:
殺 → 杀
離 → 离
雖 → 虽
親 → 亲
號 → 号
畝 → 亩
類 → 类
From the right:
務 → 务
誇 → 夸
餘 → 余
捨 → 舍
隸 → 隶
鹹 → 咸
謄 → 誊

From the middle:

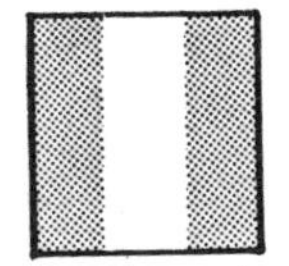

開 → 开
闢 → 辟
術 → 术

From top *and* bottom:

尋 → 寻
慮 → 虑
奪 → 夺
奮 → 奋
糞 → 粪

7 Cutting down on repeated elements or simplifying them.

Examples

蟲 → 虫
競 → 竞
澀 → 涩
纍 → 累
協 → 协
聶 → 聂
壘 → 垒
棗 → 枣
鹵 → 卤
斷 → 断
肅 → 肃
淵 → 渊

8 Replacing a number of different complex components with a simplified form common to all.

a) 又 replaces 雚，虛，𦰩，丵，奚 in the following characters:

雚 is simplified to 又 :

歡 → 欢
勸 → 劝
權 → 权
觀 → 观

𦰩 is simplified to 又 :

嘆 → 叹
漢 → 汉
艱 → 艰
難 → 难

Note these other simplifications using 又:
戲 → 戏
雞 → 鸡
對 → 对
雚
虘
𦰩
丵
奚
→ 又

b) 不 replaces 睘，褱 and 褱 in the following characters:

還 → 还
環 → 环
壞 → 坏
懷 → 怀

c) 舌 replaces 𤔔 and 啇 in the following characters:

亂 → 乱
辭 → 辞
適 → 适
敵 → 敌

d) ⺍ replaces 𦥑同 , 𦥑冂 and 𦥯 in the following characters:

興 → 兴
舉 → 举
譽 → 誉
學 → 学
覺 → 觉

简体字

Now that the general principles of simplification have been established, we proceed to fixed simplified forms (each one being unique) found in Tables 1 and 2.

Table 1 consists of independent characters which can also function as parts of other characters.

e.g.

長 → 长 (long)
張 → 张 (open up)

東 → 东 (east)
凍 → 冻 (freeze)

Table 2 shows simplified forms of radicals or components; they cannot stand alone as individual characters. For example, 言，食，金 are only simplified as 讠，饣，钅 if they form left-hand components:

言 (speech) has no simplified form, whereas

話 → 话

 (eat) has no simplified form, whereas

飯 → 饭

 (gold) has no simplified form, whereas

針 → 针

These other components cannot function at all by themselves:

戠，䜌，臤，𤇾，𦥯，糹，昜，宁，巠，睪，臨，咼

Tables 1A and **2A** are lists of Chinese characters simplified according to the stereotypes found in Tables 1 and 2.

In cases where simplified stereotypes exist for more than one component, they are simplified accordingly:

e.g. 繩 → 绳 (rope)

where 纟 is the simplified form for 糹

and 黾 is the simplified form for 黽

Table 3 draws up an exclusive list of characters whose simplifications are not derived from stereotypes. Understandably, characters from Table 3 cannot be found in Tables 1, 1A, 2 or 2A.

TABLE 1 Simplified characters which also function as stereotypes when they recur as components in other characters

几 幾	队 隊	夹 夾	两 兩	带 帶	
万 萬	双 雙	尧 堯	来 來	尝 嘗	
与 與	节 節	毕 畢	丽 麗	将 將	
广 廣	戋 戔	师 師	卤 鹵	亲 親	
门 門	龙 龍	当 當	时 時	娄 婁	
义 義	东 東	噹	佥 僉	举 舉	
马 馬	卢 盧	虫 蟲	龟 龜	聂 聶	
乡 鄉	业 業	岁 歲	犹 猶	虑 慮	
丰 豐	归 歸	岂 豈	条 條	监 監	
无 無	尔 爾	迁 遷	穷 窮	党 黨	
韦 韋	乐 樂	乔 喬	灵 靈	罢 罷	
专 專	鸟 鳥	华 華	画 畫	笔 筆	
云 雲	刍 芻	会 會	卖 賣	爱 愛	
艺 藝	汇 匯	杀 殺	齿 齒	离 離	
历 歷	彙	刘 劉	虏 虜	宾 賓	
曆	宁 寧	齐 齊	国 國	难 難	
区 區	写 寫	产 產	黾 黽	啬 嗇	
车 車	边 邊	农 農	罗 羅	断 斷	
冈 岡	发 發	寻 尋	囉	隐 隱	
贝 貝	髮	尽 盡	质 質	窜 竄	
见 見	圣 聖	儘	鱼 魚	属 屬	
气 氣	对 對	孙 孫	备 備	献 獻	
长 長	动 動	阴 陰	郑 鄭		
从 從	执 執	买 買	单 單		
仑 侖	亚 亞	寿 壽	审 審		
仓 倉	过 過	麦 麥	肃 肅		
风 風	厌 厭	进 進	录 錄		
乌 烏	页 頁	壳 殼	参 參		
为 爲	达 達	严 嚴	荐 薦		

TABLE 1A Simplified characters based on the stereotypes found in Table 1

几	闪 閃	娴 嫻	仪 儀	骂 罵	骡 騾
叽 嘰	扪 捫	阈 閾	蚁 蟻	笃 篤	骢 驄
玑 璣	闭 閉	阉 閹	**马**	骁 驍	羁 羈
机 機	问 問	阊 閶	冯 馮	骄 驕	骤 驟
矶 磯	闯 闖	阌 閿	驭 馭	骅 驊	骥 驥
虮 蟣	闰 閏	阍 閽	吗 嗎	骆 駱	骧 驤
万	闱 闈	阎 閻	犸 獁	骈 駢	**乡**
厉 厲	闲 閑	阏 閼	妈 媽	骇 駭	芗 薌
迈 邁	间 間	阐 闡	驮 馱	骊 驪	**丰**
励 勵	闵 閔	焖 燜	驯 馴	骋 騁	沣 灃
疠 癘	闷 悶	搁 擱	驰 馳	验 驗	艳 豔
虿 蠆	闸 閘	痫 癇	玛 瑪	骎 駸	滟 灩
趸 躉	闺 閨	阑 闌	驱 驅	骏 駿	**无**
砺 礪	闻 聞	阒 闃	驳 駁	骐 騏	抚 撫
蛎 蠣	闼 闥	阔 闊	驴 驢	骑 騎	芜 蕪
粝 糲	闽 閩	阕 闋	码 碼	骒 騍	呒 嘸
与	闾 閭	裥 襇	驽 駑	骓 騅	庑 廡
屿 嶼	闿 闓	榈 櫚	驾 駕	骖 驂	怃 憮
欤 歟	阀 閥	简 簡	驵 駔	骘 騭	妩 嫵
广	阁 閣	阖 闔	驶 駛	骛 騖	**韦**
邝 鄺	⿵门争 ⿵門爭	阗 闐	驸 駙	骗 騙	伟 偉
圹 壙	阂 閡	阙 闕	驷 駟	骚 騷	违 違
扩 擴	阃 閫	蔺 藺	驹 駒	骜 驁	韧 韌
犷 獷	⿵门坐 ⿵門坐	阚 闞	驺 騶	蓦 驀	苇 葦
旷 曠	阅 閱	澜 瀾	驻 駐	腾 騰	围 圍
矿 礦	阆 閬	斓 斕	驼 駝	骞 騫	帏 幃
门	润 潤	⿰口阚 ⿰口闞	驿 驛	骝 騮	玮 瑋
闩 閂	涧 澗	躏 躪	骀 駘	骟 騸	炜 煒
们 們	悯 憫	**义**	蚂 螞	骠 驃	祎 禕

Table 1A

韨 韍	奁 奩	挥 揮	堑 塹	辘 轆	贪 貪
涠 潿	呕 嘔	荤 葷	啭 囀	錾 鏨	贫 貧
韩 韓	岖 嶇	砗 硨	崭 嶄	辙 轍	贯 貫
韫 韞	沤 漚	轱 軲	渐 漸	辚 轔	贰 貳
韪 韙	怄 慪	轲 軻	惭 慚	**冈**	贲 賁
韬 韜	妪 嫗	轳 轤	皲 皸	刚 剛	贳 貰
专	枢 樞	轴 軸	辇 輦	㧏 掆	贵 貴
传 傳	瓯 甌	轶 軼	辊 輥	岗 崗	郧 鄖
抟 摶	欧 歐	轷 軤	辋 輞	㭎 棡	勋 勛
䏝 膞	殴 毆	轸 軫	椠 槧	**贝**	帧 幀
砖 磚	眍 瞘	轹 轢	暂 暫	贞 貞	贱 賤
云	躯 軀	轺 軺	辍 輟	则 則	贴 貼
芸 蕓	**车**	轻 輕	辎 輜	负 負	贶 貺
昙 曇	轧 軋	浑 渾	辈 輩	贡 貢	贻 貽
叆 靉	厍 厙	恽 惲	辉 輝	员 員	贷 貸
叇 靆	轨 軌	珲 琿	裢 褳	呗 唄	贸 貿
艺	军 軍	载 載	裈 褌	财 財	浈 湞
呓 囈	阵 陣	莲 蓮	翚 翬	狈 狽	测 測
历	轩 軒	轼 軾	毂 轂	责 責	恻 惻
坜 壢	连 連	轾 輊	辏 輳	厕 厠	费 費
苈 藶	轫 軔	轿 轎	辐 輻	贤 賢	陨 隕
呖 嚦	库 庫	辂 輅	辑 輯	败 敗	贺 賀
沥 瀝	匦 匭	较 較	输 輸	账 賬	损 損
枥 櫪	转 轉	晕 暈	辔 轡	贩 販	埙 塤
疬 癧	轭 軛	涟 漣	辕 轅	贬 貶	贽 贄
雳 靂	斩 斬	琏 璉	辖 轄	贮 貯	贾 賈
区	轮 輪	辄 輒	辗 輾	侦 偵	桢 楨
伛 傴	软 軟	辅 輔	舆 輿	侧 側	啧 嘖
抠 摳	郓 鄆	辆 輛	撵 攆	货 貨	喷 噴

Table 1A

圆 圓	喷 噴	赛 賽	岘 峴	怅 悵	舱 艙
贼 賊	遗 遺	𫌨 襀	现 現	张 張	跄 蹌
贿 賄	赋 賦	璎 瓔	规 規	枨 棖	**风**
赂 賂	𧹗 䝼	聩 聵	枧 梘	胀 脹	岚 嵐
赅 賅	赌 賭	𬑕 瞶	觅 覓	涨 漲	沨 渢
赆 贐	赎 贖	樱 櫻	视 視	**从**	枫 楓
债 債	赐 賜	篑 簣	砚 硯	苁 蓯	砜 碸
赁 賃	赒 賙	赝 贗	觇 覘	枞 樅	疯 瘋
资 資	赔 賠	豮 豶	览 覽	怂 慫	飒 颯
涢 溳	赕 賧	赠 贈	觉 覺	耸 聳	[illegible]
祯 禎	赓 賡	赞 贊	蚬 蜆	**仑**	飔 颸
琐 瑣	愤 憤	獭 獺	觊 覬	伦 倫	飕 颼
掼 摜	愦 憒	瘿 癭	笕 筧	抡 掄	飗 飀
勚 勩	溃 潰	濑 瀨	觋 覡	囵 圇	飘 飄
匮 匱	溅 濺	懒 懶	靓 靚	沦 淪	飙 飆
殒 殞	赪 赬	赡 贍	揽 攬	[illegible]	**乌**
赉 賚	赖 賴	赢 贏	搅 攪	**仓**	邬 鄔
啧 嘖	碛 磧	癞 癩	觌 覿	伧 傖	坞 塢
帻 幘	㱮 殨	攒 攢	榄 欖	创 創	呜 嗚
账 賬	赗 賵	籁 籟	觎 覦	抢 搶	**为**
婴 嬰	腻 膩	瓒 瓚	窥 窺	苍 蒼	伪 僞
赊 賒	赘 贅	臜 臢	觐 覲	呛 嗆	沩 溈
偾 僨	撄 攖	赣 贛	觏 覯	沧 滄	妫 嬀
渍 漬	槚 檟	趱 趲	觑 覷	怆 愴	**队**
惯 慣	嘤 嚶	躜 躦	**气**	玱 瑲	坠 墜
葳 蕆	赙 賻	戆 戇	忾 愾	枪 槍	**双**
蒉 蕢	罂 罌	**见**	**长**	戗 戧	[illegible]
赍 賫	赚 賺	苋 莧	伥 倀	炝 熗	**节**
赏 賞	[illegible]	觃 覎	帐 帳	疮 瘡	疖 癤

Table 1A

栉	櫛	詟	讋	栎	櫟	鸸	鴯	鹖	鶡	皱	皺
戋		**东**		烁	爍	䴕	鴷	鹗	鶚	趋	趨
刬	剗	冻	凍	砾	礫	鸹	鴰	鹘	鶻	雏	雛
浅	淺	陈	陳	**鸟**		鸺	鵂	鹙	鶖	**汇**	
栈	棧	岽	崬	鸠	鳩	鸻	鴴	鹚	鶿	[illegible]	[illegible]
残	殘	栋	棟	茑	蔦	鸼	鵃	鹛	鶥	**宁**	
盏	盞	胨	腖	鸢	鳶	鸽	鴿	鹜	鶩	拧	擰
笺	箋	**卢**		鸣	鳴	鸾	鸞	鹝	鷊	咛	嚀
践	踐	芦	蘆	鸤	鳲	䴔	鵁	鹟	鶲	狞	獰
龙		庐	廬	鸥	鷗	鸿	鴻	鹠	鶹	泞	濘
陇	隴	垆	壚	鸦	鴉	鹁	鵓	鹡	鶺	柠	檸
拢	攏	炉	爐	鸧	鶬	鹂	鸝	鹤	鶴	聍	聹
茏	蘢	泸	瀘	鸨	鴇	鹃	鵑	鹥	鷖	**写**	
垄	壟	栌	櫨	鸩	鴆	鹄	鵠	鹦	鸚	泻	瀉
咙	嚨	胪	臚	莺	鶯	鹅	鵝	鹧	鷓	**边**	
庞	龐	舻	艫	鸪	鴣	鹆	鵒	鹨	鷚	笾	籩
泷	瀧	**业**		鸫	鶇	鹈	鵜	鹩	鷯	**发**	
宠	寵	邺	鄴	鸬	鸕	鹇	鷴	鹪	鷦	拨	撥
珑	瓏	**归**		鸭	鴨	鹉	鵡	鹫	鷲	废	廢
栊	櫳	岿	巋	鸮	鴞	鹊	鵲	鹬	鷸	泼	潑
䶮	龑	**尔**		鸯	鴦	鹋	鶓	鹭	鷺	**圣**	
昽	曨	迩	邇	鸰	鴒	鹌	鵪	鹯	鸇	柽	檉
胧	朧	弥	彌	鸱	鴟	鹏	鵬	鹰	鷹	蛏	蟶
砻	礱		瀰	鸲	鴝	鹐	鵮	䴙	鸊	**对**	
聋	聾	祢	禰	鸵	鴕	鹑	鶉	鹳	鸛	怼	懟
龚	龔	玺	璽	鸳	鴛	鹒	鶊	**刍**		**动**	
袭	襲	猕	獼	[illegible]	鴪	鹕	鶘	㑇	㑳	恸	慟
笼	籠	**乐**		鸶	鷥	䴗	鶪	邹	鄒	**执**	
龛	龕	泺	濼	鸷	鷙			㤘	㥮	垫	墊

Table 1A

挚 摯	鬚	𬇙 𣸣	侠 俠	哔 嗶	侨 僑
垫 墊	顼 頊	颗 顆	陕 陝	筚 篳	挢 撟
絷 縶	顽 頑	撷 擷	挟 挾	跸 蹕	荞 蕎
亚	顿 頓	题 題	荚 莢	**师**	峤 嶠
垭 埡	倾 傾	颙 顒	峡 峽	狮 獅	娇 嬌
挜 掗	颀 頎	颛 顓	狭 狹	浉 溮	桥 橋
垩 堊	颁 頒	颜 顏	浃 浹	蛳 螄	硚 礄
哑 啞	颂 頌	额 額	硖 硤	筛 篩	矫 矯
娅 婭	颃 頏	颞 顳	惬 愜	**当**	鞒 鞽
恶 惡	烦 煩	颟 顢	蛱 蛺	挡 擋	**华**
噁	预 預	颠 顛	箧 篋	档 檔	哗 嘩
氩 氬	硕 碩	濒 瀕	瘗 瘞	裆 襠	桦 樺
壶 壺	颅 顱	颡 顙	**尧**	**虫**	晔 曄
过	领 領	颢 顥	侥 僥	蛊 蠱	烨 燁
挝 撾	庼 廎	嚣 囂	挠 撓	**岁**	**会**
厌	颇 頗	巅 巔	荛 蕘	刿 劌	侩 儈
恹 懨	颈 頸	颤 顫	哓 嘵	哕 噦	刽 劊
厣 厴	颉 頡	颥 顬	峣 嶢	秽 穢	郐 鄶
靥 靨	颊 頰	颦 顰	浇 澆	**岂**	荟 薈
魇 魘	颋 頲	癫 癲	娆 嬈	剀 剴	哙 噲
餍 饜	颌 頜	灏 灝	桡 橈	凯 凱	狯 獪
黡 黶	颍 潁	颧 顴	晓 曉	垲 塏	浍 澮
页	颏 頦	**达**	烧 燒	恺 愷	桧 檜
顶 頂	颐 頤	挞 撻	硗 磽	桤 榿	脍 膾
顷 頃	蓣 蕷	哒 噠	翘 翹	硙 磑	烩 燴
顸 頇	频 頻	𬇕 澾	蛲 蟯	皑 皚	**杀**
项 項	颓 頹	鞑 韃	跷 蹺	**迁**	**刘**
顺 順	颔 頷	**夹**	**毕**	跹 躚	浏 瀏
须 須	颖 穎	郏 郟	荜 蓽	**乔**	**齐**

Table 1A

侪 儕	逊 遜	魉 魎	睑 瞼	龅 齙	鱽 魛
剂 劑	**阴**	蹒 蹣	裣 襝	龆 齠	渔 漁
挤 擠	荫 蔭	懑 懣	签 簽	龇 齜	鱿 魷
荠 薺	**买**	**丽**	籤	龈 齦	鲁 魯
济 濟	荬 蕒	郦 酈	蔹 蘞	龉 齬	鲂 魴
脐 臍	**寿**	俪 儷	潋 瀲	龊 齪	蓟 薊
蛴 蠐	俦 儔	逦 邐	**龟**	龋 齲	鲅 鮁
跻 躋	涛 濤	酾 釃	**犹**	龌 齷	鲆 鮃
霁 霽	焘 燾	**来**	莸 蕕	**虏**	鲇 鮎
齑 齏	祷 禱	莱 萊	**条**	掳 擄	鲈 鱸
产	畴 疇	崃 崍	涤 滌	**国**	鲊 鮓
浐 滻	筹 籌	徕 徠	**穷**	掴 摑	稣 穌
萨 薩	踌 躊	涞 淶	䓖 藭	帼 幗	鲋 鮒
农	**麦**	睐 睞	**灵**	腘 膕	䲟 鮣
侬 儂	唛 嘜	**卤**	棂 欞	蝈 蟈	鲍 鮑
哝 噥	麸 麩	鹾 鹺	**画**	**黾**	鲏 鮍
浓 濃	**进**	**时**	婳 嫿	渑 澠	鲐 鮐
脓 膿	琎 璡	埘 塒	**卖**	鼋 黿	鲎 鱟
寻	**壳**	莳 蒔	渎 瀆	蝇 蠅	鲑 鮭
挦 撏	悫 慤	**佥**	椟 櫝	鼍 鼉	鲒 鮚
荨 蕁	**严**	俭 儉	犊 犢	**罗**	鲔 鮪
浔 潯	俨 儼	剑 劍	牍 牘	萝 蘿	鲖 鮦
尽	酽 釅	险 險	窦 竇	逻 邏	鲗 鰂
荩 藎	**两**	捡 撿	黩 黷	猡 玀	鲙 鱠
浕 濜	俩 倆	猃 獫	**齿**	椤 欏	鲚 鱭
烬 燼	唡 啢	检 檢	龀 齔	箩 籮	鲛 鮫
孙	满 滿	殓 殮	啮 嚙	**质**	鲜 鮮
荪 蓀	瞒 瞞	敛 斂	龃 齟	踬 躓	鲟 鱘
狲 猻	螨 蟎	脸 臉	龄 齡	**鱼**	鲞 鯗

Table 1A

鲞 鯗	鲿 鱨	鳟 鱒	**录**	嵝 嶁	尴 尷
噜 嚕	鳃 鰓	鳢 鱧	箓 籙	溇 漊	滥 濫
鲠 鯁	鳁 鰮	鳣 鱣	**参**	屡 屢	槛 檻
鲡 鱺	鳄 鰐	**备**	掺 摻	楼 樓	褴 襤
鲢 鰱	鳅 鰍	惫 憊	渗 滲	数 數	篮 籃
鲣 鰹	鳆 鰒	**郑**	惨 慘	䁖 瞜	**党**
鲥 鰣	鳇 鰉	掷 擲	毵 毿	瘘 瘻	傥 儻
鲤 鯉	䲡 鰌	踯 躑	碜 磣	窭 窶	**罢**
鲦 鰷	鳊 鯿	**单**	䅟 穇	褛 褸	摆 擺
鲧 鯀	鳌 鰲	郸 鄲	瘆 瘮	耧 耬	襬
鲩 鯇	[illegible]	掸 撣	糁 糝	蝼 螻	罴 羆
鲫 鯽	䲢 鰧	惮 憚	**荐**	篓 簍	䎬 䎱
鲨 鯊	鳍 鰭	弹 彈	鞯 韉	屦 屨	**笔**
橹 櫓	鳎 鰨	婵 嬋	**带**	擞 擻	滗 潷
鲭 鯖	鳏 鰥	殚 殫	滞 滯	薮 藪	**爱**
鲮 鯪	鳑 鰟	禅 禪	**尝**	髅 髏	嗳 噯
鲰 鯫	鳒 鰜	瘅 癉	**将**	**举**	嫒 嬡
鲱 鯡	鳖 鱉	蝉 蟬	奖 獎	榉 櫸	瑷 璦
氇 氌	鳘 鰵	箪 簞	桨 槳	**聂**	暧 曖
鲲 鯤	鳓 鰳	蕲 蘄	浆 漿	摄 攝	**离**
鲳 鯧	鳔 鰾	冁 囅	蒋 蔣	嗫 囁	漓 灕
鲵 鯢	鳕 鱈	**审**	酱 醬	滠 灄	篱 籬
鲶 鯰	鳗 鰻	婶 嬸	**亲**	慑 懾	**宾**
鲷 鯛	鳙 鱅	**肃**	榇 櫬	蹑 躡	傧 儐
鲸 鯨	鳛 鰼	萧 蕭	**娄**	**虑**	摈 擯
鲻 鯔	癣 癬	啸 嘯	偻 僂	摅 攄	滨 濱
藓 蘚	鳜 鱖	箫 簫	搂 摟	滤 濾	嫔 嬪
䲠 鰆	鳝 鱔	潇 瀟	蒌 蔞	**监**	槟 檳
鲽 鰈	鳞 鱗	蟏 蠨	喽 嘍	蓝 藍	殡 殯

Table 1A

膑 臏					
髌 髕					
鬓 鬢					
难					
傩 儺					
摊 攤					
滩 灘					
瘫 癱					
啬					
墙 墻					
蔷 薔					
嫱 嬙					
樯 檣					
穑 穡					
断					
簖 籪					
隐					
瘾 癮					
窜					
撺 攛					
蹿 躥					
属					
嘱 囑					
瞩 矚					
献					

TABLE 2 Simplified stereotypes which cannot stand alone as individual characters

讠 言					
纟 糸					
饣 食					
𠃓 昜					
〢又 臤					
宀 𡨄					
𢀖 巠					
龷 𤇾					
只 戠					
𠬤 睪					
𭕄 與					
〢𠂉 臨					
钅 金					
亦 䜌					
呙 咼					

TABLE 2A Simplified characters based on the stereotypes found in Table 2

讠	诂 詁	诡 詭	读 讀	谚 諺	谴 譴
订 訂	诃 訶	询 詢	诽 誹	谛 諦	谵 譫
计 計	评 評	诣 詣	课 課	谜 謎	辩 辯
讣 訃	诅 詛	诤 諍	诿 諉	谝 諞	雠 讎
讥 譏	识 識	该 該	谀 諛	谞 諝	霭 靄
讦 訐	诇 詗	详 詳	谁 誰	储 儲	谶 讖
讧 訌	诈 詐	诧 詫	谂 諗	谟 謨	纟
讨 討	诉 訴	诨 諢	调 調	谠 讜	纠 糾
讪 訕	诊 診	诩 詡	谄 諂	谡 謖	丝 絲
讫 訖	诋 詆	罚 罰	谅 諒	谢 謝	纡 紆
训 訓	诌 謅	狱 獄	谆 諄	谣 謠	红 紅
议 議	词 詞	浒 滸	谇 誶	谤 謗	纣 紂
讯 訊	诎 詘	诫 誡	谈 談	谥 謚	纥 紇
记 記	诏 詔	诬 誣	谊 誼	谦 謙	纨 紈
讳 諱	译 譯	语 語	谉 讅	谧 謐	约 約
讴 謳	诒 詒	诮 誚	谌 諶	谨 謹	级 級
讵 詎	诓 誆	误 誤	谋 謀	谩 謾	纩 纊
讶 訝	诔 誄	诰 誥	谍 諜	谪 謫	纪 紀
讷 訥	试 試	诱 誘	谎 謊	谫 謭	纫 紉
许 許	诖 詿	诲 誨	谏 諫	谬 謬	纬 緯
讹 訛	诗 詩	诳 誑	谐 諧	蔼 藹	纭 紜
论 論	诘 詰	说 說	谑 謔	槠 櫧	纯 純
讻 訩	诙 詼	诵 誦	谒 謁	谭 譚	纰 紕
讼 訟	诚 誠	诶 誒	谓 謂	谮 譖	纱 紗
讽 諷	诛 誅	请 請	谔 諤	谯 譙	纲 綱
设 設	话 話	诸 諸	谕 諭	谰 讕	纳 納
访 訪	诞 誕	诹 諏	谖 諼	谱 譜	纴 紝
诀 訣	诟 詬	诺 諾	谘 諮	谲 譎	纵 縱
	诠 詮	诼 諑	谙 諳	谳 讞	

Table 2A

纶 綸	荮 葤	绯 緋	缓 緩	缮 繕	饶 饒
纷 紛	哟 喲	绰 綽	缒 縋	缯 繒	蚀 蝕
纸 紙	绑 綁	绲 緄	缔 締	橼 櫞	饷 餉
纹 紋	绒 絨	绳 繩	缕 縷	缰 繮	饸 餄
纻 紵	结 結	维 維	编 編	缱 繾	饹 餎
纺 紡	绕 繞	绵 綿	缗 緡	缲 繰	饺 餃
纼 紖	绖 絰	绶 綬	缘 緣	缳 繯	饻 餏
纽 紐	绘 繪	绷 綳	缙 縉	缴 繳	饼 餅
纾 紓	绞 絞	绸 綢	缜 縝	辫 辮	饽 餑
咝 噝	统 統	绺 綹	缚 縛	缵 纘	饿 餓
线 綫	绗 絎	绻 綣	缛 縟	**饣**	馁 餒
绀 紺	给 給	综 綜	缝 縫	饥 饑	馃 餜
绁 紲	绚 絢	绽 綻	缞 縗	饦 飥	馄 餛
绂 紱	绛 絳	绾 綰	缟 縞	饧 餳	馅 餡
组 組	络 絡	绿 綠	缡 縭	饨 飩	馆 館
绅 紳	绝 絕	缀 綴	缢 縊	饩 餼	馇 餷
䌷 紬	莼 蒓	缁 緇	缣 縑	饪 飪	馈 饋
细 細	绠 綆	缂 緙	缤 繽	饫 飫	馉 餶
终 終	绡 綃	缃 緗	潍 濰	饬 飭	馊 餿
织 織	绢 絹	缄 緘	缥 縹	饭 飯	馎 餺
绉 縐	绣 綉	缅 緬	缦 縵	饮 飲	馍 饃
绊 絆	绥 綏	缆 纜	缧 縲	饯 餞	馏 餾
绋 紼	绦 縧	缇 緹	缨 纓	饰 飾	馐 饈
绌 絀	绨 綈	缈 緲	缩 縮	饱 飽	馑 饉
绍 紹	绩 績	缉 緝	缪 繆	饲 飼	馒 饅
绎 繹	绪 緒	缊 緼	缫 繅	饳 飿	馓 饊
经 經	绫 綾	缌 緦	蕴 蘊	饴 飴	馔 饌
绐 紿	续 續	缎 緞	缬 纈	饵 餌	馕 饢
荭 葒	绮 綺	缑 緱	缭 繚		**𠃓**

Table 2A

扬 揚	泾 涇	炽 熾	钓 釣	钲 鉦	铒 鉺
场 塲	氢 氫	职 職	钒 釩	钳 鉗	铓 鋩
汤 湯	胫 脛	**𠬤**	钔 鍆	钴 鈷	铔 錏
杨 楊	烃 烴	择 擇	钕 釹	钵 鉢	铗 鋏
旸 暘	痉 痙	峄 嶧	钖 鍚	钶 鈳	铙 鐃
肠 腸	羟 羥	泽 澤	钗 釵	钷 鉕	铛 鐺
炀 煬	巯 巰	怿 懌	钘 鈃	钹 鈸	铝 鋁
砀 碭	**龷**	萚 蘀	钙 鈣	钺 鉞	铜 銅
畅 暢	劳 勞	释 釋	钚 鈈	钼 鉬	铞 銱
疡 瘍	茔 塋	箨 籜	钛 鈦	钽 鉭	铟 銦
荡 蕩	茕 煢	**⺍**	[钅牙] 釾	钾 鉀	铠 鎧
殇 殤	荣 榮	峃 嶨	钝 鈍	铀 鈾	铡 鍘
烫 燙	荥 滎	学 學	钞 鈔	钿 鈿	铢 銖
觞 觴	荦 犖	喾 嚳	钡 鋇	铂 鉑	铣 銑
収	荧 熒	黉 黌	钢 鋼	铃 鈴	铥 銩
坚 堅	捞 撈	**𫩏**	钠 鈉	铄 鑠	铤 鋌
肾 腎	莹 瑩	鉴 鑒	钦 欽	铅 鉛	铧 鏵
竖 竪	唠 嘮	**钅**	钧 鈞	铆 鉚	铨 銓
紧 緊	崂 嶗	钆 釓	钤 鈐	铈 鈰	铩 鎩
悭 慳	涝 澇	钇 釔	钨 鎢	铉 鉉	铪 鉿
宀	萤 螢	针 針	钩 鉤	铊 鉈	铫 銚
伫 佇	营 營	钉 釘	钪 鈧	铋 鉍	铭 銘
苎 苧	萦 縈	钊 釗	钫 鈁	铌 鈮	铬 鉻
圣	嵘 嶸	钋 釙	钬 鈥	铍 鈹	铮 錚
陉 陘	痨 癆	钌 釕	钭 鈄	䥽 鏺	铯 銫
刭 剄	耢 耮	钍 釷	钮 鈕	铎 鐸	铰 鉸
劲 勁	蝾 蠑	钎 釺	钯 鈀	铏 鉶	铱 銥
茎 莖	**只**	钏 釧	钰 鈺	铐 銬	铲 鏟
径 徑	帜 幟	钐 釤	钱 錢	铑 銠	铳 銃

Table 2A

铵 銨	锒 鋃	锷 鍔	镖 鏢	[illegible] 钁	
银 銀	锓 鋟	锹 鍬	镗 鏜	**亦**	
铷 銣	锔 鋦	锸 鍤	镘 鏝	变 變	
衔 銜	锕 錒	锻 鍛	镚 鏰	峦 巒	
揿 撳	锗 鍺	锼 鎪	镛 鏞	弯 彎	
嵚 嶔	错 錯	锾 鍰	镜 鏡	孪 孿	
铸 鑄	锘 鍩	锵 鏘	镝 鏑	娈 孌	
铹 鐒	锚 錨	锿 鎄	镞 鏃	栾 欒	
铺 鋪	锛 錛	镀 鍍	镢 鐝	挛 攣	
铼 錸	锝 鍀	镁 鎂	镣 鐐	恋 戀	
铽 鋱	锞 錁	镂 鏤	镤 鏷	蛮 蠻	
链 鏈	锟 錕	镃 鎡	镥 鑥	脔 臠	
铿 鏗	锡 錫	镄 鐨	镦 鐓	湾 灣	
销 銷	锢 錮	镅 鎇	镧 鑭	滦 灤	
锁 鎖	锣 鑼	镊 鑷	[illegible] 鐥	銮 鑾	
锃 鋥	锤 錘	镇 鎮	镨 鐠	**呙**	
锄 鋤	锥 錐	镉 鎘	镡 鐔	剐 剮	
锂 鋰	锦 錦	镋 钂	镪 鏹	埚 堝	
锅 鍋	锧 鑕	镌 鐫	镫 鐙	莴 萵	
锆 鋯	锨 鍁	镍 鎳	镬 鑊	㖞 喎	
锇 鋨	锫 錇	镎 鎿	镭 鐳	涡 渦	
锈 銹	锭 錠	镏 鎦	镮 鐶	娲 媧	
锉 銼	键 鍵	镐 鎬	镯 鐲	脶 腡	
锋 鋒	锯 鋸	镑 鎊	镰 鐮	祸 禍	
锌 鋅	锰 錳	镒 鎰	镱 鐿	窝 窩	
锎 鐦	锱 錙	镓 鎵	镲 鑔	蜗 蝸	
锏 鐧	锲 鍥	镔 鑌	镳 鑣		
锐 鋭	锴 鍇	[illegible] 鍽	镴 鑞		
锑 銻	锶 鍶	[illegible] 鐯	镶 鑲		

TABLE 3 Simplified characters which have not been derived from any stereotype

厂 廠	习 習	苏 囌	烂 爛	忧 憂	阳 陽
卜 蔔	折 摺	协 協	头 頭	扰 擾	远 遠
仆 僕	开 開	胁 脅	礼 禮	伤 傷	园 園
扑 撲	合 閤	邓 鄧	出 齣	价 價	运 運
朴 樸	关 關	劝 勸	础 礎	阶 階	坛 壇
补 補	板 闆	欢 歡	台 臺	伙 夥	罎
儿 兒	辟 闢	观 觀	颱	向 嚮	坏 壞
了 瞭	厅 廳	戏 戲	檯	响 響	怀 懷
疗 療	听 聽	艰 艱	巩 鞏	后 後	坝 壩
辽 遼	币 幣	书 書	筑 築	众 衆	坟 墳
干 乾	仅 僅	击 擊	扫 掃	爷 爺	获 獲
幹	叹 嘆	陆 陸	妇 婦	伞 傘	穫
赶 趕	汉 漢	术 術	压 壓	杂 雜	护 護
亏 虧	权 權	灭 滅	夸 誇	凫 鳧	沪 滬
才 纔	凤 鳳	旧 舊	夺 奪	袅 裊	块 塊
谗 讒	斗 鬥	帅 帥	奋 奮	枭 梟	声 聲
搀 攙	闹 鬧	叶 葉	划 劃	岛 島	报 報
馋 饞	阄 鬮	号 號	尘 塵	捣 搗	拟 擬
千 韆	阋 鬩	电 電	吁 籲	壮 壯	克 剋
忏 懺	认 認	只 隻	吓 嚇	装 裝	极 極
纤 縴	让 讓	祇	虾 蝦	庄 莊	医 醫
纖	讲 講	积 積	曲 麯	妆 妝	还 還
歼 殲	证 證	丛 叢	面 麵	状 狀	环 環
亿 億	征 徵	处 處	团 團	寝 寢	县 縣
忆 憶	症 癥	冬 鼕	糰	冲 衝	悬 懸
个 個	惩 懲	务 務	回 迴	庆 慶	里 裏
么 麼	丑 醜	兰 蘭	网 網	灯 燈	缠 纏
卫 衞	办 辦	拦 攔	朱 硃	兴 興	吨 噸
飞 飛	苏 蘇	栏 欄	优 優	导 導	邮 郵

Table 3

困 睏	层 層	舍 捨	毡 氈	昼 晝	袜 襪
别 彆	迟 遲	籴 糴	选 選	垒 壘	剧 劇
乱 亂	际 際	肤 膚	宪 憲	蚕 蠶	据 據
辞 辭	标 標	肮 骯	秋 鞦	盐 鹽	继 繼
敌 敵	鸡 雞	庙 廟	复 復	壶 壺	梦 夢
适 適	表 錶	疟 瘧	複	桩 樁	酝 醞
刮 颳	势 勢	卷 捲	覆	赃 贓	累 纍
体 體	热 熱	宝 寶	胜 勝	脏 臟	偿 償
佣 傭	亵 褻	帘 簾	独 獨	髒	衅 釁
拥 擁	拣 揀	实 實	浊 濁	样 樣	盘 盤
痈 癰	练 練	衬 襯	烛 燭	痒 癢	猎 獵
彻 徹	炼 煉	隶 隸	触 觸	顾 顧	蜡 蠟
余 餘	担 擔	帮 幫	养 養	毙 斃	腊 臘
谷 穀	胆 膽	赵 趙	姜 薑	致 緻	旋 鏇
邻 鄰	苹 蘋	茧 繭	类 類	钻 鑽	盖 蓋
怜 憐	范 範	药 藥	粪 糞	称 稱	兽 獸
岭 嶺	柜 櫃	树 樹	总 總	借 藉	渊 淵
系 係	松 鬆	咸 鹹	洼 窪	舰 艦	淀 澱
繫	胡 鬍	牵 牽	洁 潔	胶 膠	惧 懼
亩 畝	丧 喪	战 戰	洒 灑	斋 齋	惊 驚
应 應	枣 棗	点 點	晒 曬	准 準	琼 瓊
这 這	矾 礬	临 臨	牺 犧	竞 競	堕 墮
灿 燦	态 態	显 顯	恼 惱	递 遞	随 隨
灶 竈	轰 轟	虽 雖	脑 腦	涂 塗	椭 橢
沟 溝	图 圖	钟 鐘	窃 竊	涩 澀	郁 鬱
构 構	制 製	鍾	袄 襖	宽 寬	粜 糶
购 購	迭 疊	种 種	跃 躍	家 傢	联 聯
沈 瀋	铁 鐵	肿 腫	垦 墾	象 像	确 確
启 啓	凭 憑	钥 鑰	恳 懇	窍 竅	硷 鹼

Table 3

鑿	凿
禦	御
濕	湿
饗	飨
矇 濛 懞	蒙
礙	碍
霧	雾
謄	誊
譽	誉
糧	粮
衊	蔑
釀	酿
願	愿
踴	踊
穩	稳
聰	聪
黴	霉
髖	髋

APPENDIX A

A word of caution! However tempting it may be to pounce upon stereotypes (those found in Tables 1 and 2) and simplify all characters accordingly, very likely it would prove a totally frustrating process because exceptions occur in many cases.

Having chosen a few characters and components, we proceed to show how and when such exceptions arise, if only to impress upon the reader the utter complexity of the Chinese script he has to deal with!

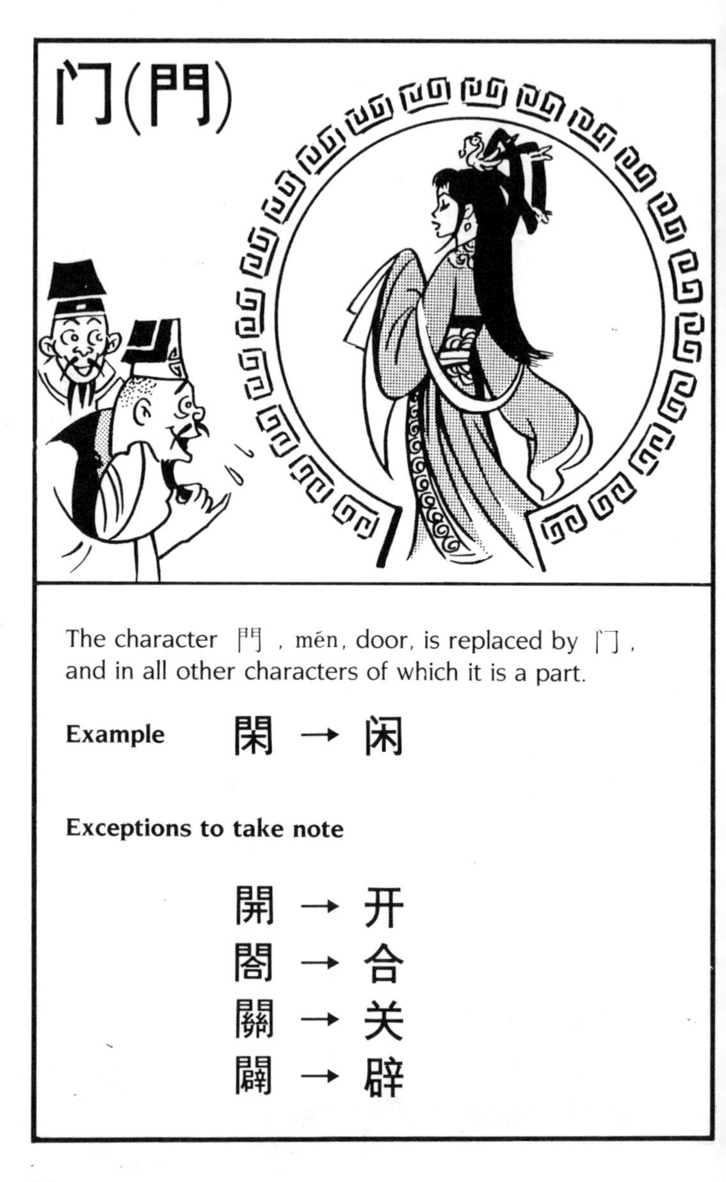

The character 門, mēn, door, is replaced by 门, and in all other characters of which it is a part.

Example 閑 → 闲

Exceptions to take note

開 → 开
閤 → 合
關 → 关
闢 → 辟

闆 → 板
蘭 → 兰
欄 → 栏
攔 → 拦
爛 → 烂

As for these 3 characters, their regular form does not involve 門 but 鬥, the 'fight' radical. The simplified form of 鬥 as a separate character is 斗

鬧 → 闹
鬩 → 阋
鬮 → 阄

鸟(鳥)

The character 鳥, niǎo, bird, is replaced by 鸟, and in all other characters of which it is a part. 鸟(鳥) should not be confused with 乌(烏), the difference being only a stroke.

Examples

on the right: 鷗 → 鸥

at the bottom: 鷹 → 鹰

Exceptions to take note

The top component is brought to the side.

鷥 → 鸶

The straight line which normally replaces the 4 dots is omitted altogether.

鳧 → 凫

As for these 2 characters, the 4 dots are absent from the regular form.

梟 → 枭
裊 → 袅

In this other instance, the 鳥 component does not appear in the regular character, though it does in its simplified form.

雞 → 鸡

The character 魚, yú, fish, is replaced by 鱼, and in all other characters of which it is a part. A straight line replaces the four dots.

Examples

on the left:	鮮	→	鲜
on the right:	漁	→	渔
at the bottom:	鯊	→	鲨
on top:	魯	→	鲁
or even:	艣	→	橹

Exceptions to take note

蘇 → 苏
囌 → 苏

The character 貝, bèi, cowrie, is replaced by 贝, and in all other characters of which it is a part.

Examples

on the left: 財 → 财

at the bottom: 貪 → 贪

on top: 櫻 → 樱

in the middle: 側 → 侧

or even: 圓 → 圆

慣 → 惯

賴 → 赖

Exceptions to take note

價 → 价

墳 → 坟

櫃 → 柜

實 → 实

鑽 → 钻

積 → 积

償 → 偿

買 → 买

賣 → 卖

In this other instance, the 貝 component does not appear in the regular character, though it does in its simplified form.

壩 → 坝

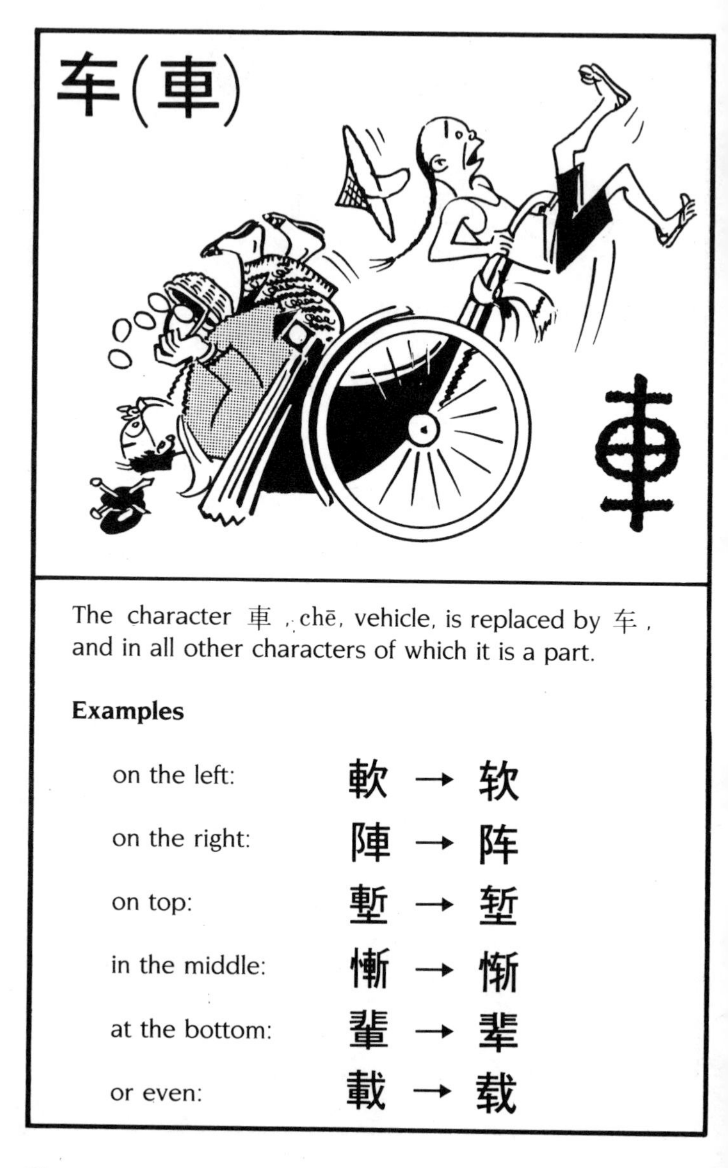

The character 車, chē, vehicle, is replaced by 车, and in all other characters of which it is a part.

Examples

on the left:	軟	→	软
on the right:	陣	→	阵
on top:	塹	→	堑
in the middle:	慚	→	惭
at the bottom:	輩	→	辈
or even:	載	→	载

Exceptions to take note

範 → 范
運 → 运

Only the top 車 is simplified.

轟 → 轰

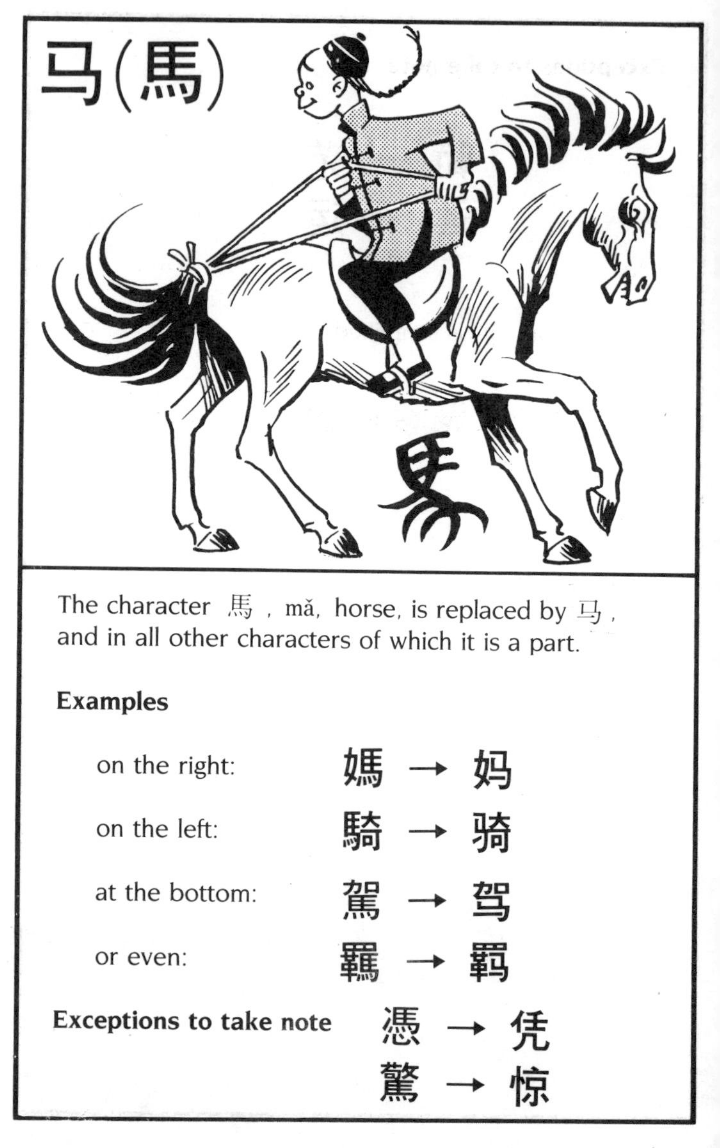

The character 馬, mǎ, horse, is replaced by 马, and in all other characters of which it is a part.

Examples

on the right:	媽	→	妈
on the left:	騎	→	骑
at the bottom:	駕	→	驾
or even:	羈	→	羁

Exceptions to take note

憑 → 凭

驚 → 惊

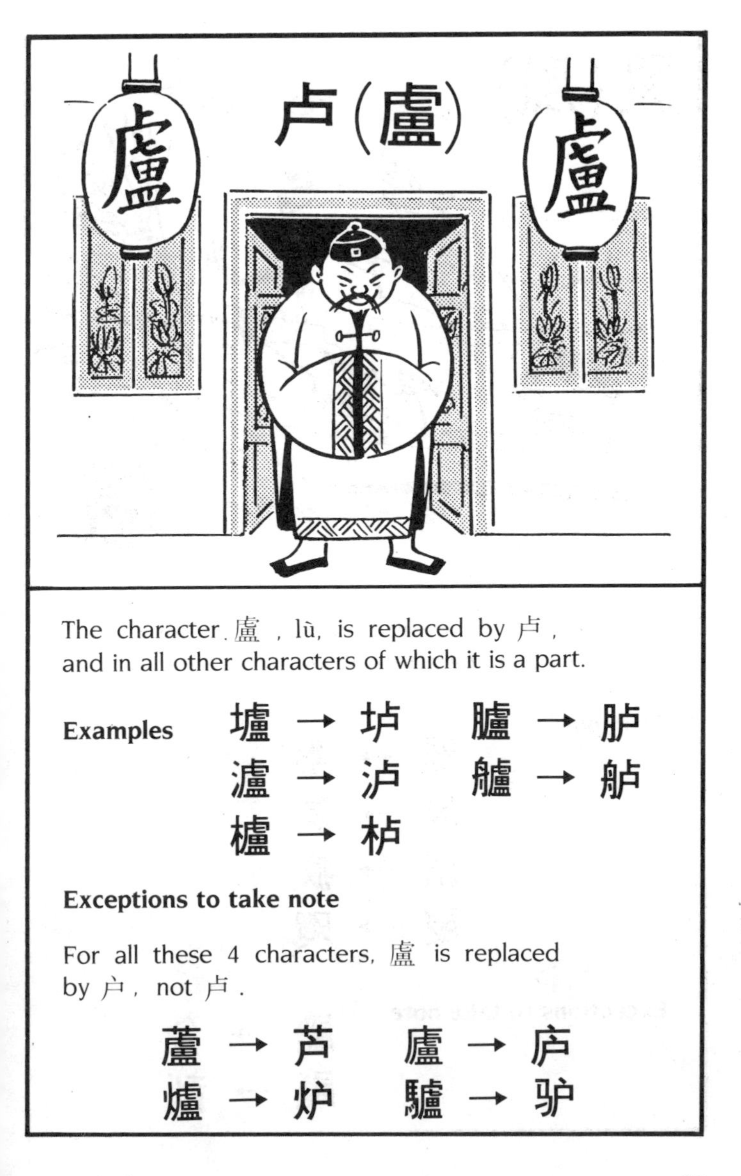

The character 盧, lǜ, is replaced by 卢, and in all other characters of which it is a part.

Examples

壚 → 垆　　臚 → 胪
瀘 → 泸　　艫 → 舻
櫨 → 栌

Exceptions to take note

For all these 4 characters, 盧 is replaced by 户, not 卢.

蘆 → 芦　　廬 → 庐
爐 → 炉　　驢 → 驴

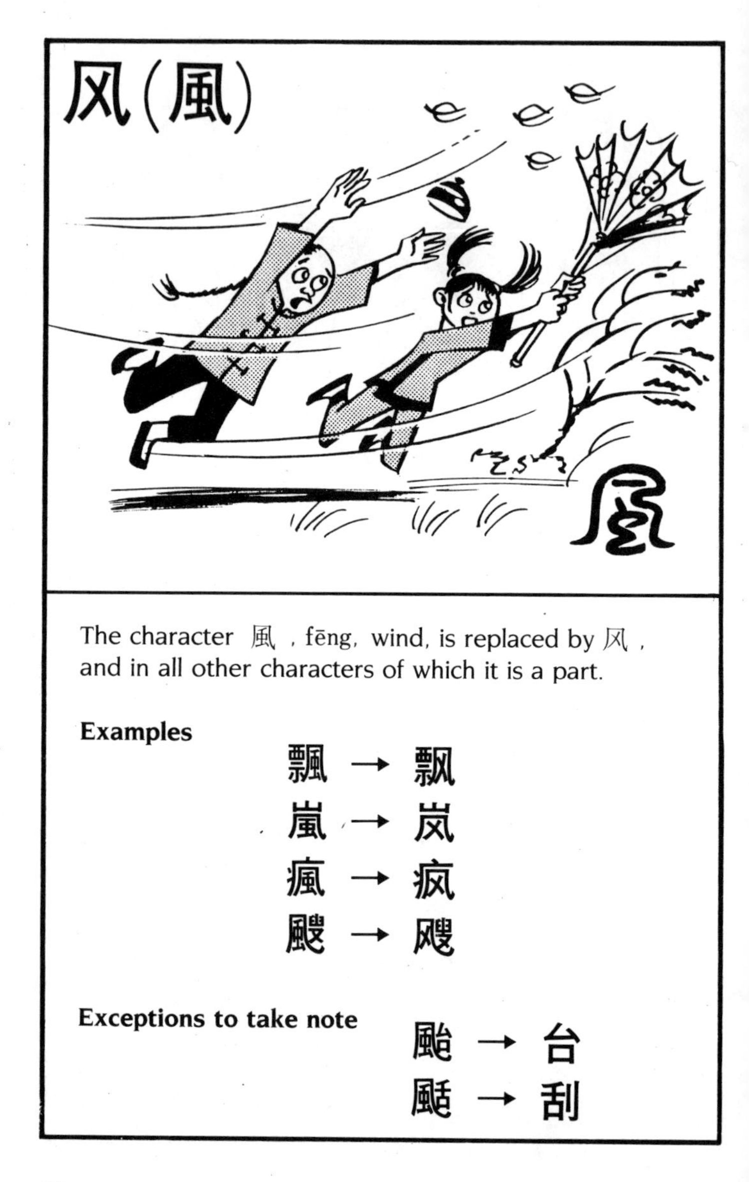

风(風)

The character 風, fēng, wind, is replaced by 风, and in all other characters of which it is a part.

Examples

飄 → 飘
嵐 → 岚
瘋 → 疯
颼 → 飕

Exceptions to take note

颱 → 台
颳 → 刮

将(將)

The character 將, jiāng, be about to, is replaced by 将, and if it should be part of another character.

Example 蔣 → 蒋

Exceptions to take note

When 將 occurs at the top, the 寸 component is omitted.

奬 → 奖

槳 → 桨

漿 → 浆

醬 → 酱

The component 昜 is replaced by 𠃓, and affects all characters of which it is a part.

Examples

瘍 → 疡
燙 → 烫
觴 → 觞

Exceptions to take note

In this instance, the 𠂉 element is removed in the simplified character.

場 → 场

A revision of ideas explains these 2 simplifications.

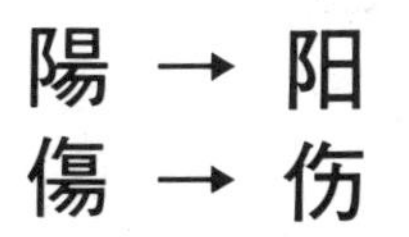

讠(言)

The 'speech' radical 言 is replaced by 讠, and affects all characters of which it is a part. It occurs mostly on the left.

Examples

話 → 话
譏 → 讥
罰 → 罚
辯 → 辩

Exceptions to take note

In the following characters, the 'speech' radical is simplified as usual, but the right-hand components, though having no simplified stereotypes, are simplified according to a phonetic principle or otherwise.

認 → 认
讓 → 让
講 → 讲
證 → 证
讒 → 谗

In this instance, the 'speech' radical gives way to the 'hand' radical.

護 → 护

Here the 'speech' radical is dropped out of sight.

誇 → 夸

Look at how these have been simplified:

譽 → 誉　　這 → 这
讋 → 詟　　膽 → 胆

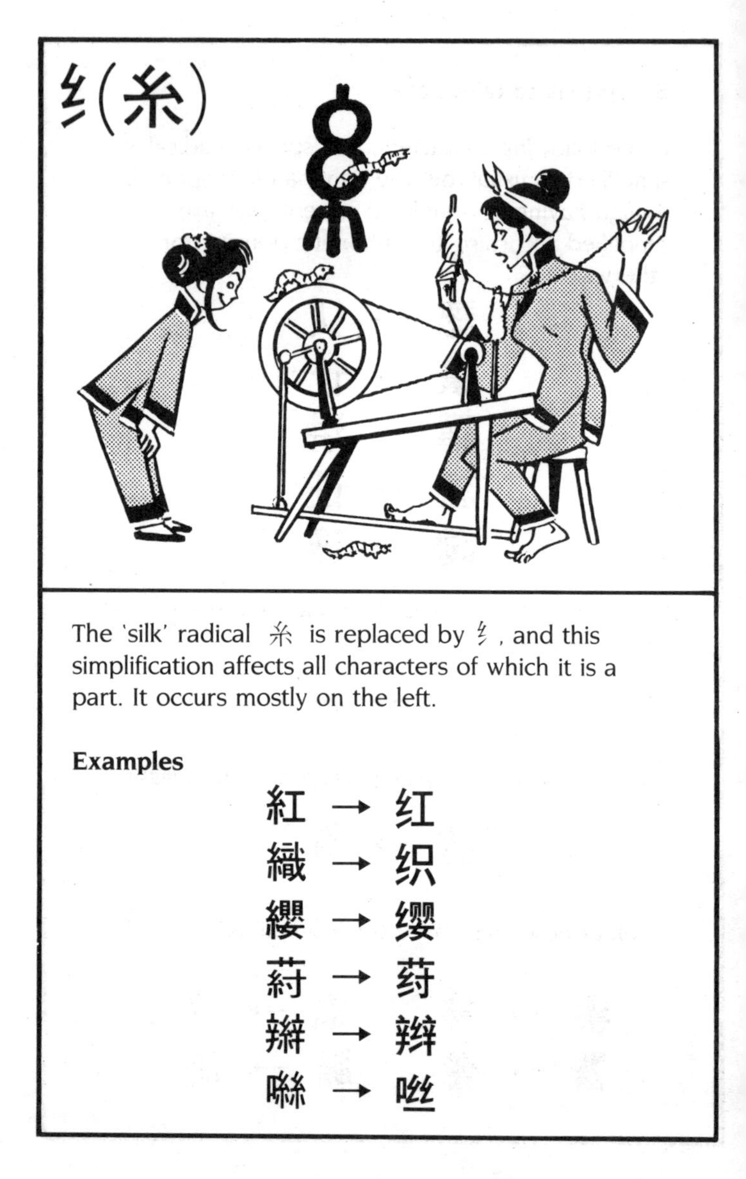

纟(糸)

The 'silk' radical 糸 is replaced by 纟, and this simplification affects all characters of which it is a part. It occurs mostly on the left.

Examples

紅 → 红
織 → 织
纓 → 缨
葤 → 荮
辮 → 辫
噝 → 咝

Exceptions to take note

In the following characters, the 'silk' radical is simplified as usual, but the right-hand components, though having no simplified stereotypes, are simplified according to a phonetic principle or otherwise:

The 'silk' radical disappears altogether in these other simplifications:

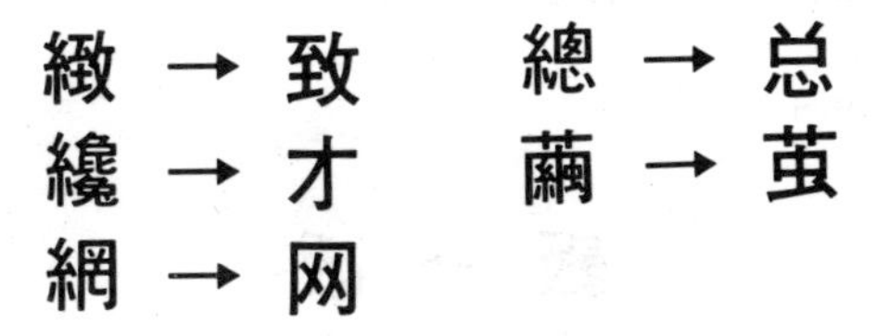

Here, the 糸 component does not appear in the regular character, though it does in its simplified form.

藥 → 药

The 'food' radical 食 is replaced by 饣, but only if it occurs on the left-hand side.

Examples

飯 → 饭
餞 → 饯

Exceptions to take note

Although the 'food' radical on the left is simplified as usual, the right-hand element is given a simplified form which is *not* to be regarded as a stereotype:

饞 → 馋

Here the 'food' radical is omitted:

餘 → 余

钅(金)

The 'gold' radical 金 is replaced by 钅, and this simplification affects all characters of which it is a part. More often than not, it is found on the left.

Examples

針 → 针
錢 → 钱
銜 → 衔
撳 → 揿
嶔 → 嵚

Exceptions to take note

In the following characters, the 'gold' radical is simplified as usual, but the right-hand components have been given simplified forms *not* to be taken as stereotypes.

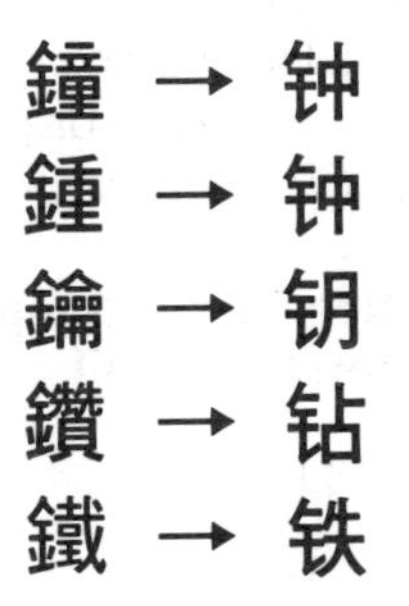

These other simplified forms have had the 'gold' radical omitted:

Look at how these have been simplified:

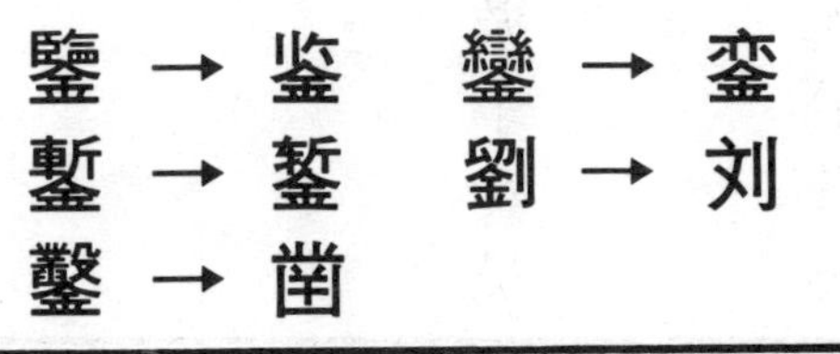

APPENDIX B

Apart from the lists of simplified Chinese characters found in Tables 1, 1A, 2A and 3, there are others which had already undergone changes from their original forms earlier, and have been accepted into the body of commonly used regular characters. The original forms were gradually displaced from present-day usage over a period of time.

Earlier form	Regular form	Simplified form (if any)
掛	挂	
朶	朵	
異	异	
淨	净	
淚	泪	
貓	猫	
豬	猪	
棄	弃	
牆	墙	
閒	閑	闲
遊	游	
於	于	
黃	黄	
吳	吴	

APPENDIX C

During the simplification process, some of the elements are subtly modified, and can be easily missed if not careful. As they are not isolated in Tables 1 or 2 as stereotypes to be followed, it is useful here to provide a reference list.

e.g. a regular character like 賴 is simplified to 赖, where 贝 is the simplified form for 貝. But note also that 刀 has been changed to ⺈.

Hence, 賴 → 赖

Regular element	Simplified element
亐	亏
务	务
県	县
呂	吕
𠬶	𠬷
扁	扁
夕	爫
兪	俞
示	礻
眞	真

Regular element	Simplified element
彔	录
者	者
产	产
凡	卂
処	处
令	令
𥁕	昷
辶	辶
曾	曾
虛	虚
滿	满
骨	骨

APPENDIX D

Remarkable similarities exist among some of the simplified forms. Their regular forms are enclosed in brackets.

Examples

风 (風)
凤 (鳳)

从 (從)
丛 (叢)

鸟 (鳥)
乌 (烏)

与 (與)
写 (寫)

冈 (岡)
网 (網)

东 (東)
乐 (樂)

刍 (芻)
当 (當)

广 (廣)
厂 (廠)

A Hanyu Pinyin list of Simplified and Regular Characters

A 爱

Pinyin	Simplified	Regular
ā	锕	錒
āi	锿	鎄
ái	皑	皚
ǎi	霭	靄
āi	嗳	噯
ǎi	嗳	噯
ài	嗳	噯
ǎi	蔼	藹
ài	爱	愛
ài	叆	靉
ài	瑷	璦
ài	暧	曖
ài	嫒	嬡
ài	碍	礙
ān	谙	諳
ān	鹌	鵪
ǎn	铵	銨
āng	肮	骯
áo	鳌	鰲
ǎo	袄	襖
ào	骜	驁

B 鳊

Pinyin	Simplified	Regular
bǎ	钯	鈀
bà	鲅	鮁
bà	坝	壩
bà	罢	罷
ba	罢	罷
bà	䎱	䎬
bǎi	摆	擺
		襬
bài	败	敗
bān	颁	頒
bǎn	板	闆
bàn	绊	絆
bàn	办	辦
bāng	帮	幫
bǎng	绑	綁
bàng	谤	謗
bàng	镑	鎊
bāo	龅	齙
bǎo	宝	寶
bǎo	饱	飽
bǎo	鸨	鴇
bào	报	報
bào	鲍	鮑
bèi	惫	憊
bèi	辈	輩
bèi	贝	貝
bèi	钡	鋇
bèi	狈	狽
bèi	备	備
bei	呗	唄
bēn	锛	錛
bēn	贲	賁
bēng	绷	綳
běng	绷	綳
bèng	镚	鏰
bǐ	笔	筆
bì	铋	鉍
bì	贲	賁
bì	毕	畢
bì	哔	嗶
bì	筚	篳
bì	荜	蓽
bì	跸	蹕
bì	滗	潷
bì	币	幣
bì	闭	閉
bì	毙	斃
biān	鳊	鯿
biān	编	編
biān	边	邊
biān	笾	籩
biǎn	贬	貶
biàn	辩	辯
biàn	辫	辮
biàn	变	變
biāo	镳	鑣
biāo	标	標
biāo	骠	驃

biāo	镖	鏢
biāo	飙	飆
biǎo	表	錶
biào	鳔	鰾
biē	鳖	鱉
biē	瘪	癟
biě	瘪	癟
biè	别	彆
bīn	宾	賓
bīn	滨	濱
bīn	槟	檳
bīn	傧	儐
bīn	缤	繽
bīn	镔	鑌
bīn	濒	瀕
bìn	鬓	鬢
bìn	摈	擯
bìn	殡	殯
bìn	膑	臏
bìn	髌	髕
bīng	槟	檳
bǐng	饼	餅
bō	饽	餑
bō	钵	鉢
bō	拨	撥
bó	鹁	鵓
bó	馎	餺
bó	钹	鈸
bó	驳	駁
bó	铂	鉑
bo	卜	蔔
bǔ	补	補
bù	钚	鈈

C 车

cái	才	纔
cái	财	財
cān	参	參
cān	骖	驂
cán	蚕	蠶
cán	惭	慚
cán	残	殘
cǎn	惨	慘
cǎn	䅟	穇
càn	灿	燦
cāng	仓	倉
cāng	沧	滄
cāng	苍	蒼
cāng	伧	傖
cāng	鸧	鶬
cāng	舱	艙
cè	测	測
cè	恻	惻
cè	厕	厠
cè	侧	側
cēn	参	參
cēng	层	層
chā	馇	餷
chā	锸	鍤
chǎ	镲	鑔
chà	诧	詫
chāi	钗	釵
chái	侪	儕
chài	虿	蠆
chān	搀	攙
chān	掺	摻
chán	缠	纏
chán	单	單
chán	禅	禪
chán	蝉	蟬
chán	婵	嬋
chán	谗	讒
chán	馋	饞
chǎn	产	產
chǎn	浐	滻
chǎn	铲	鏟
chǎn	蒇	蕆
chǎn	阐	闡
chǎn	冁	囅
chǎn	谄	諂
chàn	颤	顫
chàn	忏	懺
chàn	刬	剗
chǎn	刬	剗
chāng	伥	倀

chāng	阊	閶	chēng	称	稱	chú	雏	雛
chāng	鲳	鯧	chèng	称	稱	chǔ	储	儲
cháng	尝	嘗	chéng	枨	棖	chǔ	础	礎
cháng	偿	償	chéng	诚	誠	chǔ	处	處
cháng	鲿	鱨	chéng	惩	懲	chù	处	處
cháng	长	長	chěng	骋	騁	chù	绌	絀
cháng	肠	腸	chī	鸱	鴟	chù	触	觸
cháng	场	場	chí	迟	遲	chuài	[illegible]	[illegible]
chǎng	场	場	chí	驰	馳	chuán	传	傳
chǎng	厂	廠	chǐ	齿	齒	chuàn	钏	釧
chàng	怅	悵	chì	炽	熾	chuāng	疮	瘡
chàng	畅	暢	chì	饬	飭	chuǎng	闯	闖
chāo	钞	鈔	chōng	冲	衝	chuáng	闯	闖
chē	车	車	chòng	冲	衝	chuáng	怆	愴
chē	砗	硨	chóng	虫	蟲	chuáng	创	創
chè	彻	徹	chǒng	宠	寵	chuāng	创	創
chén	谌	諶	chòng	铳	銃	chuí	锤	錘
chén	尘	塵	chōu	䌷	紬	chūn	䲠	鰆
chén	陈	陳	chòu	䌷	紬	chún	鹑	鶉
chěn	碜	磣	chóu	畴	疇	chún	纯	純
chèn	榇	櫬	chóu	筹	籌	chún	莼	蒓
chèn	衬	襯	chóu	踌	躊	chuò	绰	綽
chèn	谶	讖	chóu	俦	儔	chuò	龊	齪
chèn	称	稱	chóu	雠	讎	chuò	辍	輟
chèn	龀	齔	chóu	绸	綢	cí	鹚	鶿
chēng	柽	檉	chǒu	丑	醜	cí	辞	辭
chēng	蛏	蟶	chū	出	齣	cí	词	詞
chēng	铛	鐺	chú	锄	鋤	cì	赐	賜
chēng	赪	赬	chú	刍	芻	cōng	聪	聰

cōng	骢	驄
cōng	枞	樅
cōng	苁	蓯
cōng	从	從
cóng	从	從
cóng	丛	叢
còu	辏	輳
cuān	撺	攛
cuān	蹿	躥
cuān	镩	鑹
cuán	攒	攢
cuàn	窜	竄
cuī	缞	縗
cuó	鹾	鹺
cuò	错	錯
cuò	锉	銼

D
灯

dá	达	達
dá	哒	噠
dá	鞑	韃
dài	贷	貸
dài	绐	紿
dài	带	帶
dài	叇	靆
dān	单	單
dān	担	擔
dàn	担	擔
dān	殚	殫
dān	箪	簞
dān	郸	鄲
dǎn	掸	撣
dǎn	胆	膽
dǎn	赕	賧
dàn	惮	憚
dàn	瘅	癉
dàn	弹	彈
dàn	诞	誕
dāng	裆	襠
dāng	铛	鐺
dāng	当	當
dàng	当	當
dāng	当	噹
dǎng	党	黨
dǎng	谠	讜
dǎng	挡	擋
dàng	挡	擋
dàng	档	檔
dàng	砀	碭
dàng	荡	蕩
dāo	鱽	魛
dǎo	祷	禱
dǎo	岛	島
dǎo	捣	搗
dǎo	导	導
dē	锝	鍀
dēng	灯	燈
dèng	镫	鐙
dèng	邓	鄧
dī	镝	鏑
dí	镝	鏑
dí	觌	覿
dí	籴	糴
dí	敌	敵
dí	涤	滌
dǐ	诋	詆
dì	谛	諦
dì	缔	締
dì	递	遞
diān	颠	顛
diān	癫	癲
diān	巅	巔
diǎn	点	點
diàn	淀	澱
diàn	垫	墊
diàn	电	電
diàn	钿	鈿
diāo	鲷	鯛
diào	铫	銚
diào	铞	銱
diào	窎	窵
diào	钓	釣
diào	调	調
dié	谍	諜
dié	鲽	鰈

dié	绖	絰
dié	迭	疊
dīng	钉	釘
dìng	钉	釘
dǐng	顶	頂
dìng	订	訂
dìng	锭	錠
diū	铥	銩
dōng	东	東
dōng	鸫	鶇
dōng	岽	崬
dōng	冬	鼕
dòng	动	動
dòng	冻	凍
dòng	栋	棟
dòng	胨	腖
dǒu	钭	鈄
dòu	斗	鬥
dòu	窦	竇
dòu	读	讀
dú	读	讀
dú	渎	瀆
dú	椟	櫝
dú	黩	黷
dú	犊	犢
dú	牍	牘
dú	独	獨
dǔ	赌	賭
dǔ	笃	篤

dù	镀	鍍
duàn	断	斷
duàn	锻	鍛
duàn	缎	緞
duàn	簖	籪
duì	怼	懟
duì	对	對
duì	队	隊
duì	镦	鐓
duī	镦	鐓
dūn	吨	噸
dūn	镦	鐓
dǔn	趸	躉
dùn	钝	鈍
dùn	顿	頓
duó	夺	奪
duó	铎	鐸
duò	驮	馱
duò	堕	墮
duò	饳	飿

E
鳄

é	额	額
é	锇	鋨
é	鹅	鵝
é	讹	訛
ě	恶	惡
è	恶	噁
è	垩	堊
è	轭	軛
è	谔	諤
è	鹗	鶚
è	鳄	鰐
è	锷	鍔
è	饿	餓
ē	诶	誒
é	诶	誒
ě	诶	誒
è	诶	誒
ér	儿	兒
ér	鸸	鴯
ěr	饵	餌
ěr	铒	鉺
ěr	尔	爾
ěr	迩	邇
èr	贰	貳

F
饭

fā	发	發
fà		髮
fá	罚	罰
fá	阀	閥
fán	烦	煩
fán	矾	礬

fán	钒	釩
fàn	贩	販
fàn	饭	飯
fàn	范	範
fāng	钫	鈁
fáng	鲂	魴
fǎng	访	訪
fǎng	纺	紡
fēi	绯	緋
fēi	鲱	鯡
fēi	飞	飛
fěi	诽	誹
fèi	废	廢
fèi	费	費
fèi	镄	鐨
fēn	纷	紛
fén	坟	墳
fén	豮	豶
fèn	粪	糞
fèn	愤	憤
fèn	偾	僨
fèn	奋	奮
fēng	丰	豐
fēng	沣	灃
fēng	锋	鋒
fēng	风	風
fēng	沨	渢
fēng	疯	瘋
fēng	枫	楓

fēng	砜	碸
féng	冯	馮
féng	缝	縫
fèng	缝	縫
fěng	讽	諷
fèng	凤	鳳
fèng	赗	賵
fū	麸	麩
fū	肤	膚
fú	辐	輻
fú	韨	韍
fú	绂	紱
fú	凫	鳧
fú	绋	紼
fǔ	辅	輔
fǔ	抚	撫
fù	赋	賦
fù	赙	賻
fù	缚	縛
fù	讣	訃
fù	复	復
		複
		覆
fù	鳆	鰒
fù	驸	駙
fù	鲋	鮒
fù	负	負
fù	妇	婦

G 龟

gā	夹	夾
gá	钆	釓
gāi	该	該
gāi	赅	賅
gài	盖	蓋
gài	钙	鈣
gān	干	乾
gàn	干	幹
gān	尴	尷
gǎn	赶	趕
gàn	赣	贛
gàn	绀	紺
gāng	冈	岡
gāng	刚	剛
gāng	㭎	棡
gāng	纲	綱
gāng	钢	鋼
gàng	钢	鋼
gāng	㧏	掆
gāng	岗	崗
gǎng	岗	崗
gǎo	镐	鎬
gǎo	缟	縞
gào	诰	誥
gào	锆	鋯

gē	鸽	鴿
gē	纥	紇
gē	搁	擱
gé	搁	擱
gé	镉	鎘
gé	颌	頜
gé	阁	閣
gě	盖	蓋
gě	个	個
gè	个	個
gè	铬	鉻
gěi	给	給
gēng	赓	賡
gēng	鹒	鶊
gěng	鲠	鯁
gěng	绠	綆
gōng	龚	龔
gōng	红	紅
gǒng	巩	鞏
gòng	贡	貢
gòng	唝	嗊
gōu	缑	緱
gōu	沟	溝
gōu	钩	鈎
gòu	觏	覯
gòu	诟	詬
gòu	构	構
gòu	购	購
gū	轱	軲
gū	鸪	鴣
gǔ	诂	詁
gǔ	钴	鈷
gǔ	贾	賈
gǔ	蛊	蠱
gǔ	毂	轂
gǔ	馉	餶
gǔ	鹘	鶻
gǔ	谷	穀
gǔ	鹄	鵠
gù	顾	顧
gù	锢	錮
guā	刮	颳
guā	鸹	鴰
guǎ	剐	剮
guá	诖	詿
guān	关	關
guān	纶	綸
guān	鳏	鰥
guān	观	觀
guàn	观	觀
guǎn	馆	館
guàn	鹳	鸛
guàn	贯	貫
guàn	惯	慣
guàn	掼	摜
guǎng	广	廣
guǎng	犷	獷
guī	妫	嬀
guī	沩	潙
guī	规	規
guī	鲑	鮭
guī	闺	閨
guī	归	歸
guī	龟	龜
guǐ	轨	軌
guǐ	匦	匭
guǐ	诡	詭
guì	鳜	鱖
guì	柜	櫃
guì	贵	貴
guì	刿	劌
guì	桧	檜
guì	刽	劊
gǔn	辊	輥
gǔn	绲	緄
gǔn	鲧	鯀
guō	涡	渦
guō	埚	堝
guō	锅	鍋
guō	蝈	蟈
guó	国	國
guó	掴	摑
guó	帼	幗
guó	腘	膕
guǒ	馃	餜
guō	过	過
guò	过	過

H 画

hā	铪	鉿
hái	还	還
hài	骇	駭
hān	顸	頇
hán	韩	韓
hǎn	阚	闞
hǎn	㘎	𡅅
hàn	汉	漢
hàn	颔	頷
háng	绗	絎
háng	颃	頏
hào	颢	顥
hào	灏	灝
hào	号	號
háo	号	號
hào	镐	鎬
hē	诃	訶
hé	阂	閡
hé	阖	闔
hé	鹖	鶡
hé	颌	頜
hé	饸	餄
hé	合	閤
hé	纥	紇
hè	鹤	鶴

hè	贺	賀
hè	吓	嚇
hēng	鸻	鴴
hōng	轰	轟
hóng	黉	黌
hóng	鸿	鴻
hóng	红	紅
hóng	荭	葒
hòng	讧	訌
hòu	后	後
hòu	鲎	鱟
hū	轷	軤
hú	壶	壺
hú	胡	鬍
hú	鹕	鶘
hú	鹄	鵠
hú	鹘	鶻
hǔ	浒	滸
hù	沪	滬
hù	护	護
huá	华	華
huà	华	華
huá	骅	驊
huá	哗	嘩
huā	哗	嘩
huá	铧	鏵
huà	画	畫
huà	婳	嫿
huà	划	劃

huà	桦	樺
huà	话	話
huái	怀	懷
huài	坏	壞
huān	欢	歡
huán	还	還
huán	环	環
huán	缳	繯
huán	镮	鐶
huán	锾	鍰
huǎn	缓	緩
huàn	鲩	鯇
huáng	鳇	鰉
huǎng	谎	謊
huī	挥	揮
huī	辉	輝
huī	珲	琿
huī	翚	翬
huī	诙	詼
huí	回	迴
huì	汇	匯 / 彙
huì	贿	賄
huì	秽	穢
huì	会	會
huì	桧	檜
huì	烩	燴
huì	荟	薈
huì	绘	繪

huì	诲	誨
huì	㱮	殨
huì	讳	諱
hūn	荤	葷
hūn	阍	閽
hún	浑	渾
hún	珲	琿
hún	馄	餛
hùn	诨	諢
huǒ	钬	鈥
huǒ	伙	夥
huò	镬	鑊
huò	获	獲
		穫
huò	祸	禍
huò	货	貨

J
鸡

jī	齑	齏
jī	跻	躋
jī	击	擊
jī	赍	賫
jī	缉	緝
jī	积	積
jī	羁	羈
jī	机	機
jī	饥	饑
jī	讥	譏
jī	玑	璣
jī	矶	磯
jī	叽	嘰
jī	绩	績
jī	鸡	雞
jí	鹡	鶺
jí	辑	輯
jí	极	極
jí	级	級
jí	诘	詰
jǐ	挤	擠
jǐ	给	給
jǐ	几	幾
jī	几	幾
jǐ	虮	蟣
jǐ	济	濟
jì	济	濟
jì	霁	霽
jì	荠	薺
jì	剂	劑
jì	鲚	鱭
jì	际	際
jì	计	計
jì	系	繫
jì	骥	驥
jì	觊	覬
jì	蓟	薊
jì	鲫	鯽
jì	记	記
jì	纪	紀
jǐ	纪	紀
jì	继	繼
jiā	家	傢
jiā	镓	鎵
jiā	夹	夾
jiá	夹	夾
jiā	浃	浹
jiá	颊	頰
jiá	荚	莢
jiá	蛱	蛺
jiá	铗	鋏
jiá	郏	郟
jiǎ	贾	賈
jiǎ	槚	檟
jiǎ	钾	鉀
jià	价	價
jià	驾	駕
jiān	鹣	鶼
jiān	鳒	鰜
jiān	缣	縑
jiān	戋	戔
jiān	笺	箋
jiān	坚	堅
jiān	鲣	鰹
jiān	缄	緘
jiān	鞯	韉
jiān	监	監

jiàn	监	監	jiàn	舰	艦	jiǎo	矫	矯
jiān	歼	殲	jiàn	剑	劍	jiǎo	搅	攪
jiān	艰	艱	jiàn	键	鍵	jiǎo	缴	繳
jiān	间	間	jiàn	涧	澗	jiào	觉	覺
jiàn	间	間	jiàn	锏	鐧	jiào	较	較
jiǎn	谫	謭	jiǎn	锏	鐧	jiào	轿	轎
jiǎn	硷	鹼	jiāng	姜	薑	jiào	挢	撟
jiǎn	拣	揀	jiāng	将	將	jiào	峤	嶠
jiǎn	笕	筧	jiáng	将	將	jiē	阶	階
jiǎn	茧	繭	jiāng	浆	漿	jiē	疖	癤
jiǎn	检	檢	jiàng	浆	漿	jié	讦	訐
jiǎn	捡	撿	jiāng	缰	韁	jié	洁	潔
jiǎn	睑	瞼	jiǎng	讲	講	jié	诘	詰
jiǎn	俭	儉	jiǎng	桨	槳	jié	撷	擷
jiǎn	裥	襇	jiǎng	奖	獎	jié	颉	頡
jiǎn	简	簡	jiǎng	蒋	蔣	jié	结	結
jiàn	谏	諫	jiàng	酱	醬	jiē	结	結
jiàn	渐	漸	jiàng	绛	絳	jié	鲒	鮚
jiān	渐	漸	jiāo	胶	膠	jié	节	節
jiàn	槛	檻	jiāo	鲛	鮫	jiē	节	節
jiàn	贱	賤	jiāo	䴔	鵁	jiè	借	藉
jiàn	溅	濺	jiāo	浇	澆	jiè	诫	誡
jiān	溅	濺	jiāo	骄	驕	jie	价	價
jiàn	践	踐	jiāo	娇	嬌	jǐn	谨	謹
jiàn	饯	餞	jiāo	鹪	鷦	jǐn	馑	饉
jiàn	荐	薦	jiǎo	饺	餃	jǐn	紧	緊
jiàn	鉴	鑒	jiǎo	铰	鉸	jǐn	锦	錦
jiàn	见	見	jiǎo	绞	絞	jǐn	仅	僅
jiàn	枧	梘	jiǎo	侥	僥	jìn	觐	覲

jìn	劲	勁
jìn	进	進
jìn	琎	璡
jìn	缙	縉
jìn	尽	盡
jǐn		儘
jìn	浕	濜
jìn	荩	藎
jìn	赆	贐
jìn	烬	燼
jīng	惊	驚
jīng	鲸	鯨
jīng	䴖	鶄
jīng	泾	涇
jīng	茎	莖
jīng	经	經
jǐng	颈	頸
jǐng	刭	剄
jìng	镜	鏡
jìng	竞	競
jìng	痉	痙
jìng	劲	勁
jìng	胫	脛
jìng	径	徑
jìng	靓	靚
jiū	纠	糾
jiū	鸠	鳩
jiū	阄	鬮
jiù	鹫	鷲

jiū	旧	舊
jū	车	車
jū	驹	駒
jú	䴗	鶪
jú	锔	鋦
jǔ	举	櫸
jǔ	龃	齟
jǔ	榉	舉
jù	讵	詎
jù	惧	懼
jù	飓	颶
jù	窭	窶
jù	屦	屨
jù	据	據
jū	据	據
jù	剧	劇
jù	锯	鋸
jū	锯	鋸
juān	鹃	鵑
juān	镌	鐫
juǎn	卷	捲
juàn	绢	絹
jué	觉	覺
jué	镢	鐝
jué	钁	钁
jué	谲	譎
jué	诀	訣
jué	绝	絕
jūn	军	軍

jūn	皲	皸
jūn	龟	龜
jūn	钧	鈞
jùn	骏	駿

K 宽

kāi	开	開
kāi	锎	鐦
kǎi	恺	愷
kǎi	垲	塏
kǎi	剀	剴
kǎi	铠	鎧
kǎi	凯	凱
kǎi	闿	闓
kǎi	锴	鍇
kài	忾	愾
kān	龛	龕
kǎn	槛	檻
kàn	阚	闞
kàng	钪	鈧
kào	铐	銬
kē	颏	頦
kē	轲	軻
kē	钶	鈳
kē	颗	顆
ké	壳	殼
kè	缂	緙

kè	克	剋
kè	课	課
kè	骒	騍
kè	锞	錁
kěn	恳	懇
kěn	垦	墾
kēng	铿	鏗
kōu	抠	摳
kōu	眍	瞘
kù	库	庫
kù	裤	褲
kù	喾	嚳
kuā	夸	誇
kuǎi	㧟	擓
kuài	会	會
kuài	浍	澮
kuài	哙	噲
kuài	郐	鄶
kuài	侩	儈
kuài	脍	膾
kuài	鲙	鱠
kuài	狯	獪
kuài	块	塊
kuān	宽	寬
kuān	髋	髖
kuāng	诓	誆
kuáng	诳	誑
kuàng	矿	礦
kuàng	圹	壙
kuàng	旷	曠
kuàng	纩	纊
kuàng	邝	鄺
kuàng	贶	貺
kuī	窥	窺
kuī	亏	虧
kuī	岿	巋
kuì	溃	潰
kuì	𫌀	䙌
kuì	愦	憒
kuì	聩	聵
kuì	匮	匱
kuì	蒉	蕢
kuì	馈	饋
kuì	篑	簣
kūn	鲲	鯤
kūn	锟	錕
kūn	壸	壼
kǔn	阃	閫
kùn	困	睏
kuò	阔	闊
kuò	扩	擴

L 龙

là	蜡	蠟
là	腊	臘
là	镴	鑞
lái	来	來
lái	涞	淶
lái	莱	萊
lái	崃	崍
lái	铼	錸
lái	徕	徠
lài	赖	賴
lài	濑	瀨
lài	癞	癩
lài	籁	籟
lài	睐	睞
lài	赉	賚
lán	兰	蘭
lán	栏	欄
lán	拦	攔
lán	阑	闌
lán	澜	瀾
lán	谰	讕
lán	斓	斕
lán	镧	鑭
lán	褴	襤
lán	蓝	藍
lán	篮	籃
lán	岚	嵐
lǎn	懒	懶
lǎn	览	覽
lǎn	榄	欖
lǎn	揽	攬
lǎn	缆	纜

làn	烂	爛
làn	滥	濫
láng	锒	鋃
làng	阆	閬
lāo	捞	撈
láo	劳	勞
láo	崂	嶗
láo	痨	癆
láo	铹	鐒
lǎo	铑	銠
lào	涝	澇
lào	唠	嘮
lào	耢	耮
lào	络	絡
lè	鳓	鰳
lè	乐	樂
le	饹	餎
léi	镭	鐳
léi	缧	縲
léi	累	纍
lěi	累	纍
lèi	累	纍
lěi	诔	誄
lěi	垒	壘
lèi	类	類
lí	离	離
lí	漓	灕
lí	篱	籬
lí	缡	縭
lí	骊	驪
lí	鹂	鸝
lí	鲡	鱺
lǐ	礼	禮
lǐ	逦	邐
lǐ	里	裏
lǐ	锂	鋰
lǐ	鲤	鯉
lǐ	鳢	鱧
lí	丽	麗
lì	丽	麗
lì	俪	儷
lì	郦	酈
lì	厉	厲
lì	励	勵
lì	砾	礫
lì	历	歷
		曆
lì	沥	瀝
lì	坜	壢
lì	疬	癧
lì	雳	靂
lì	枥	櫪
lì	苈	藶
lì	呖	嚦
lì	疠	癘
lì	粝	糲
lì	砺	礪
lì	蛎	蠣
lì	栎	櫟
lì	轹	轢
lì	隶	隸
liǎ	俩	倆
lián	帘	簾
lián	镰	鐮
lián	联	聯
lián	连	連
lián	涟	漣
lián	莲	蓮
lián	鲢	鰱
lián	奁	奩
lián	怜	憐
liǎn	琏	璉
liǎn	敛	斂
liǎn	脸	臉
liàn	蔹	蘞
liàn	恋	戀
liàn	链	鏈
liàn	炼	煉
liàn	练	練
liàn	潋	瀲
liàn	殓	殮
liàn	裣	襝
lian	裢	褳
liáng	粮	糧
liǎng	两	兩
liǎng	俩	倆
liǎng	唡	啢

liǎng	魉	魎
liàng	谅	諒
liàng	辆	輛
liáo	鹩	鷯
liáo	缭	繚
liáo	疗	療
liáo	辽	遼
liǎo	了	瞭
liào	了	瞭
liǎo	钌	釕
liào	钌	釕
liào	镣	鐐
liè	猎	獵
liè	䴕	鴷
lín	辚	轔
lín	鳞	鱗
lín	临	臨
lín	邻	鄰
lìn	蔺	藺
lìn	躏	躪
lìn	赁	賃
líng	鲮	鯪
líng	绫	綾
líng	龄	齡
líng	铃	鈴
líng	鸰	鴒
líng	灵	靈
líng	棂	櫺
lǐng	领	領
lǐng	岭	嶺
liú	飗	飀
liú	刘	劉
liú	浏	瀏
liú	骝	騮
liú	镏	鎦
liǔ	绺	綹
liú	馏	餾
liù	馏	餾
liù	鹨	鷚
liù	陆	陸
lóng	龙	龍
lóng	泷	瀧
lóng	珑	瓏
lóng	聋	聾
lóng	栊	櫳
lóng	砻	礱
lóng	笼	籠
lǒng	笼	籠
lóng	茏	蘢
lóng	咙	嚨
lóng	昽	曨
lóng	胧	朧
lǒng	垄	壟
lǒng	拢	攏
lǒng	陇	隴
lōu	䁖	瞜
lou	娄	婁
lóu	娄	婁
lóu	偻	僂
lóu	喽	嘍
lóu	楼	樓
lóu	溇	漊
lóu	蒌	蔞
lóu	髅	髏
lóu	蝼	螻
lóu	耧	耬
lōu	搂	摟
lǒu	搂	摟
lǒu	嵝	嶁
lǒu	篓	簍
lòu	瘘	瘻
lòu	镂	鏤
lū	噜	嚕
lú	庐	廬
lú	炉	爐
lú	芦	蘆
lú	卢	盧
lú	泸	瀘
lú	垆	壚
lú	栌	櫨
lú	颅	顱
lú	鸬	鸕
lú	胪	臚
lú	鲈	鱸
lú	舻	艫
lǔ	卤	鹵
		滷

lǔ	虏	虜
lǔ	掳	擄
lǔ	鲁	魯
lǔ	橹	櫓
lǔ	镥	鑥
lù	辘	轆
lù	辂	輅
lù	赂	賂
lù	鹭	鷺
lù	陆	陸
lù	录	錄
lù	箓	籙
lù	绿	綠
lu	轳	轤
lu	氇	氌
lǘ	驴	驢
lǘ	闾	閭
lǘ	榈	櫚
lǚ	屡	屢
lǚ	偻	僂
lǚ	褛	褸
lǚ	缕	縷
lǚ	铝	鋁
lǜ	虑	慮
lǜ	滤	濾
lǜ	绿	綠
luán	娈	孌
luán	栾	欒
luán	滦	灤
luán	峦	巒
luán	脔	臠
luán	銮	鑾
luán	挛	攣
luán	鸾	鸞
luán	孪	孿
luàn	乱	亂
lūn	抡	掄
lún	抡	掄
lún	仑	侖
lún	沦	淪
lún	轮	輪
lún	囵	圇
lún	纶	綸
lún	伦	倫
lún	论	論
lùn	论	論
luó	骡	騾
luó	脶	腡
luó	罗	羅
luō		囉
luo		囉
luó	逻	邏
luó	萝	蘿
luó	锣	鑼
luó	箩	籮
luó	椤	欏
luó	猡	玀
luò	荦	犖
luò	泺	濼
luò	骆	駱
luò	络	絡

M 梦

ḿ	呒	嘸
mā	唛	嘜
mā	妈	媽
mǎ	马	馬
mǎ	玛	瑪
mǎ	码	碼
mǎ	犸	獁
má	吗	嗎
mǎ	吗	嗎
ma	吗	嗎
mā	蚂	螞
mǎ	蚂	螞
mà	蚂	螞
mà	骂	罵
mǎi	买	買
mài	麦	麥
mài	卖	賣
mài	迈	邁
mai	荬	蕒
mān	颟	顢
mán	馒	饅
mán	鳗	鰻

mán	蛮	蠻
mán	瞒	瞞
mǎn	满	滿
mǎn	螨	蟎
mán	谩	謾
màn	谩	謾
màn	缦	縵
màn	镘	鏝
máng	铓	鋩
máo	锚	錨
mǎo	铆	鉚
mào	贸	貿
me	么	麼
méi	霉	黴
méi	镅	鎇
méi	鹛	鶥
měi	镁	鎂
mén	门	門
mén	扪	捫
mén	钔	鍆
mèn	懑	懣
mēn	闷	悶
mèn	闷	悶
mèn	焖	燜
mén	们	們
mēng	蒙	矇
méng		濛
měng		懞
měng	锰	錳
mèng	梦	夢
mí	谜	謎
mí	祢	禰
mí	弥	彌
		瀰
mí	猕	獼
mì	谧	謐
mì	觅	覓
mián	绵	綿
miǎn	渑	澠
miǎn	缅	緬
miàn	面	麵
miáo	鹋	鶓
miǎo	缈	緲
miào	缪	繆
miào	庙	廟
miè	灭	滅
miè	蔑	衊
mín	缗	緡
mǐn	闵	閔
mǐn	悯	憫
mǐn	闽	閩
mǐn	黾	黽
mǐn	鳘	鰵
míng	鸣	鳴
míng	铭	銘
miù	谬	謬
miù	缪	繆
mō	谟	謨
mó	馍	饃
mò	蓦	驀
móu	谋	謀
móu	缪	繆
mǔ	亩	畝
mù	钼	鉬

N 鸟

ná	镎	鎿
nà	钠	鈉
nà	纳	納
nán	难	難
nàn	难	難
nǎng	馕	饢
náo	挠	撓
náo	蛲	蟯
náo	铙	鐃
nǎo	恼	惱
nǎo	脑	腦
nào	闹	鬧
nè	讷	訥
něi	馁	餒
ní	鲵	鯢
ní	铌	鈮
nǐ	拟	擬
nì	腻	膩
nián	鲇	鮎

nián	鲶	鯰
niǎn	辇	輦
niǎn	撵	攆
niàng	酿	釀
niǎo	鸟	鳥
niǎo	茑	蔦
niǎo	袅	裊
niè	聂	聶
niè	颞	顳
niè	嗫	囁
niè	蹑	躡
niè	镊	鑷
niè	啮	嚙
niè	镍	鎳
níng	宁	寧
nìng	宁	寧
níng	柠	檸
níng	咛	嚀
níng	狞	獰
níng	聍	聹
níng	拧	擰
nǐng	拧	擰
nìng	拧	擰
nìng	泞	濘
niǔ	钮	鈕
niǔ	纽	紐
nóng	农	農
nóng	浓	濃
nóng	侬	儂
nóng	脓	膿
nóng	哝	噥
nú	驽	駑
nǚ	钕	釹
nüè	疟	瘧
nuó	傩	儺
nuò	诺	諾
nuò	锘	鍩

O
鸥

ōu	区	區
ōu	讴	謳
ōu	瓯	甌
ōu	鸥	鷗
ōu	殴	毆
ōu	欧	歐
ǒu	呕	嘔
ōu	沤	漚
òu	沤	漚
òu	怄	慪

P
喷

pán	蹒	蹣
pán	盘	盤
páng	鳑	鰟
páng	庞	龐
péi	赔	賠
péi	锫	錇
pèi	辔	轡
pēn	喷	噴
pèn	喷	噴
péng	鹏	鵬
pī	纰	紕
pí	罴	羆
pí	鲏	鮍
pí	铍	鈹
pì	辟	闢
pì	䴙	鸊
pián	骈	駢
piǎn	谝	諞
piàn	骗	騙
piāo	飘	飄
piāo	缥	縹
piào	骠	驃
pín	嫔	嬪
pín	频	頻
pín	颦	顰
pín	贫	貧
píng	评	評
píng	苹	蘋
píng	鲆	鮃
píng	凭	憑
pō	钋	釙
pō	颇	頗

pō	泼	潑
pō	钹	鏺
pǒ	钷	鉕
pū	铺	鋪
pù	铺	鋪
pū	扑	撲
pú	仆	僕
pú	镤	鏷
pǔ	谱	譜
pǔ	镨	鐠
pǔ	朴	樸

Q 桥

qī	缉	緝
qī	桤	榿
qí	齐	齊
qí	蛴	蠐
qí	脐	臍
qí	骑	騎
qí	骐	騏
qí	鳍	鰭
qí	颀	頎
qí	蕲	蘄
qǐ	启	啓
qǐ	绮	綺
qǐ	岂	豈
qì	碛	磧
qì	气	氣
qì	讫	訖
qi	荠	薺
qiān	骞	騫
qiān	谦	謙
qiān	悭	慳
qiān	牵	牽
qiān	佥	僉
qiān	签	簽
		籤
qiān	千	韆
qiān	迁	遷
qiān	钎	釺
qiān	铅	鉛
qiān	鸽	鴿
qián	荨	蕁
qián	钳	鉗
qián	钱	錢
qián	钤	鈐
qiǎn	浅	淺
qiǎn	谴	譴
qiǎn	缱	繾
qiàn	堑	塹
qiàn	椠	槧
qiàn	纤	縴
qiāng	玱	瑲
qiāng	枪	槍
qiāng	锵	鏘
qiáng	墙	墻
qiáng	蔷	薔
qiáng	樯	檣
qiáng	嫱	嬙
qiǎng	镪	鏹
qiǎng	羟	羥
qiǎng	抢	搶
qiàng	炝	熗
qiàng	戗	戧
qiàng	跄	蹌
qiàng	呛	嗆
qiāng	呛	嗆
qiāo	硗	磽
qiāo	跷	蹺
qiāo	锹	鍬
qiāo	缲	繰
qiáo	翘	翹
qiào	翘	翹
qiáo	乔	喬
qiáo	桥	橋
qiáo	硚	礄
qiáo	侨	僑
qiáo	轿	轎
qiáo	荞	蕎
qiáo	峤	嶠
qiáo	谯	譙
qiào	壳	殼
qiào	窍	竅
qiào	诮	誚
qiè	锲	鍥

qiè	惬	愜
qiè	箧	篋
qiè	窃	竊
qīn	亲	親
qìn	亲	親
qīn	钦	欽
qīn	嵚	嶔
qīn	骎	駸
qǐn	寝	寢
qǐn	锓	鋟
qìn	揿	撳
qīng	鲭	鯖
qīng	轻	輕
qīng	氢	氫
qīng	倾	傾
qíng	䞍	䝼
qǐng	请	請
qǐng	顷	頃
qǐng	庼	廎
qìng	庆	慶
qióng	穷	窮
qióng	䓖	藭
qióng	琼	瓊
qióng	茕	煢
qiū	秋	鞦
qiū	鹙	鶖
qiū	鳅	鰍
qiū	龟	龜
qiú	鲉	鮋
qiú	巯	巰
qū	曲	麯
qū	区	區
qū	驱	驅
qū	岖	嶇
qū	躯	軀
qū	诎	詘
qū	趋	趨
qú	鸲	鴝
qǔ	龋	齲
qù	觑	覷
qù	阒	闃
quán	权	權
quán	颧	顴
quán	铨	銓
quán	诠	詮
quǎn	绻	綣
quàn	劝	勸
què	悫	愨
què	鹊	鵲
què	阙	闕
què	确	確
què	阕	闋

R 热

ràng	让	讓
ráo	桡	橈
ráo	荛	蕘
ráo	饶	饒
ráo	娆	嬈
rǎo	娆	嬈
rǎo	扰	擾
rǎo	绕	繞
rào	绕	繞
rè	热	熱
rèn	认	認
rèn	饪	飪
rèn	纴	紝
rèn	轫	軔
rèn	纫	紉
rèn	韧	韌
róng	荣	榮
róng	蝾	蠑
róng	嵘	嶸
róng	绒	絨
rú	铷	銣
rú	颥	顬
rù	缛	縟
ruǎn	软	軟
ruì	锐	銳
rùn	闰	閏
rùn	润	潤

S 伞

sǎ	洒	灑	shàn	缮	繕	shěn	谂	諗
sà	飒	颯	shàn	掸	撣	shèn	肾	腎
sà	萨	薩	shàn	单	單	shèn	渗	滲
sāi	鳃	鰓	shàn	骟	騸	shèn	瘆	瘮
sài	赛	賽	shàn	⿰钅扇	⿰釒扇	shēng	声	聲
sān	毵	毿	shàn	禅	禪	shéng	渑	澠
sǎn	馓	饊	shàn	讪	訕	shéng	绳	繩
sǎn	伞	傘	shàn	赡	贍	shēng	胜	勝
sāng	丧	喪	shāng	殇	殤	shèng	胜	勝
sǎng	颡	顙	shāng	觞	觴	shèng	圣	聖
sāo	骚	騷	shāng	伤	傷	shī	湿	濕
sāo	缫	繅	shǎng	赏	賞	shī	诗	詩
sǎo	扫	掃	shāo	烧	燒	shī	师	師
sào	扫	掃	shào	绍	紹	shī	浉	溮
sè	涩	澀	shē	赊	賒	shī	狮	獅
sè	啬	嗇	shě	舍	捨	shī	䴓	鳾
sè	穑	穡	shè	设	設	shí	实	實
sè	铯	銫	shè	滠	灄	shí	埘	塒
shā	鲨	鯊	shè	慑	懾	shí	鲥	鰣
shā	纱	紗	shè	摄	攝	shí	识	識
shā	杀	殺	shè	厍	厙	shí	时	時
shā	铩	鎩	shéi	谁	誰	shí	蚀	蝕
shāi	筛	篩	shēn	绅	紳	shǐ	驶	駛
shài	晒	曬	shēn	参	參	shì	铈	鈰
shān	钐	釤	shēn	糁	糝	shì	视	視
shǎn	陕	陝	shěn	审	審	shì	谥	謚
shǎn	闪	閃	shěn	谉	讅	shì	试	試
shàn	⿰钅善	鐥	shěn	婶	嬸	shì	轼	軾
shàn	鳝	鱔	shěn	沈	瀋	shì	势	勢

shì	莳	蒔
shì	贳	貰
shì	释	釋
shì	饰	飾
shì	适	適
shòu	兽	獸
shòu	寿	壽
shòu	绶	綬
shū	枢	樞
shū	摅	攄
shū	输	輸
shū	纾	紓
shū	书	書
shú	赎	贖
shǔ	属	屬
shǔ	数	數
shù	数	數
shù	树	樹
shù	术	術
shù	竖	豎
shuài	帅	帥
shuān	闩	閂
shuāng	双	雙
shuāng	泷	瀧
shuí	谁	誰
shùn	顺	順
shuō	说	說
shuò	硕	碩
shuò	烁	爍
shuò	铄	鑠
sī	锶	鍶
sī	飔	颸
sī	酾	釃
sī	缌	緦
sī	丝	絲
sī	咝	噝
sī	鸶	鷥
sī	蛳	螄
sì	驷	駟
sì	饲	飼
si	厕	廁
sōng	松	鬆
sǒng	怂	慫
sǒng	耸	聳
sǒng	㧐	㩳
sòng	讼	訟
sòng	颂	頌
sòng	诵	誦
sōu	馊	餿
sōu	锼	鎪
sōu	飕	颼
sǒu	薮	藪
sǒu	擞	擻
sòu	擞	擻
sū	苏	蘇
sū	稣	穌
sù	谡	謖
sù	诉	訴
sù	肃	肅
suī	虽	雖
suí	随	隨
suí	绥	綏
suì	岁	歲
suì	谇	誶
sūn	孙	孫
sūn	荪	蓀
sūn	狲	猻
sǔn	损	損
suǒ	缩	縮
suǒ	琐	瑣
suǒ	唢	嗩
suǒ	锁	鎖
suo	苏	囌

T 头

tā	铊	鉈
tǎ	鳎	鰨
tǎ	獭	獺
tà	㳠	澾
tà	挞	撻
tà	闼	闥
tái	台	臺
		颱
		檯
tái	骀	駘

tāi	鲐	鮐
tài	态	態
tài	钛	鈦
tān	滩	灘
tān	瘫	癱
tān	摊	攤
tān	贪	貪
tán	谈	談
tán	坛	壇
		罎
tán	谭	譚
tán	昙	曇
tán	弹	彈
tǎn	钽	鉭
tàn	叹	嘆
tāng	镗	鏜
tāng	汤	湯
tǎng	傥	儻
tǎng	镋	鎲
tàng	烫	燙
tāo	涛	濤
tāo	韬	韜
tāo	绦	縧
tāo	焘	燾
tǎo	讨	討
tè	铽	鋱
téng	誊	謄
téng	腾	騰
téng	[illegible]	黱
tī	锑	銻
tī	䴘	鷉
tí	鹈	鵜
tí	绨	綈
tì	绨	綈
tí	缇	緹
tí	题	題
tǐ	体	體
tián	阗	闐
tián	钿	鈿
tiáo	条	條
tiáo	鲦	鰷
tiáo	龆	齠
tiáo	调	調
tiào	粜	糶
tiē	贴	貼
tiě	铁	鐵
tīng	厅	廳
tīng	烃	烴
tīng	听	聽
tǐng	颋	頲
tǐng	铤	鋌
tóng	铜	銅
tóng	鲖	鮦
tǒng	统	統
tòng	恸	慟
tóu	头	頭
tú	图	圖
tú	涂	塗
tǔ	钍	釷
tuán	抟	摶
tuán	团	團
		糰
tuí	颓	頹
tún	饨	飩
tuō	饦	飥
tuó	驼	駝
tuó	鸵	鴕
tuó	驮	馱
tuó	鼍	鼉
tuǒ	椭	橢
tuò	萚	蘀
tuò	箨	籜

W 纹

wā	娲	媧
wā	洼	窪
wà	袜	襪
wāi	㖞	喎
wān	弯	彎
wān	湾	灣
wán	纨	紈
wán	顽	頑
wǎn	绾	綰
wàn	万	萬
wǎng	网	網

Pinyin	Simplified	Traditional
wǎng	辋	輞
wéi	为	爲
wèi	为	爲
wéi	维	維
wéi	潍	濰
wéi	韦	韋
wéi	违	違
wéi	围	圍
wéi	涠	潿
wéi	帏	幃
wéi	闱	闈
wěi	伪	僞
wěi	鲔	鮪
wěi	诿	諉
wěi	炜	煒
wěi	玮	瑋
wěi	苇	葦
wěi	韪	韙
wěi	伟	偉
wěi	纬	緯
wèi	硙	磑
wèi	谓	謂
wèi	卫	衞
wēn	鳁	鰮
wén	纹	紋
wén	闻	聞
wén	阌	閿
wěn	稳	穩
wèn	问	問
wō	涡	渦
wō	窝	窩
wō	莴	萵
wō	蜗	蝸
wō	挝	撾
wò	龌	齷
wū	诬	誣
wū	乌	烏
wū	呜	嗚
wū	钨	鎢
wū	邬	鄔
wú	无	無
wú	芜	蕪
wǔ	妩	嫵
wǔ	怃	憮
wǔ	庑	廡
wǔ	鹉	鵡
wù	恶	惡
wù	坞	塢
wù	务	務
wù	雾	霧
wù	骛	騖
wù	鹜	鶩
wù	误	誤
xī	牺	犧
xī	铱	餏
xī	锡	錫
xí	袭	襲
xí	觋	覡
xí	习	習
xí	鳛	鰼
xǐ	玺	璽
xǐ	铣	銑
xì	系	係
		繫
xì	细	細
xì	阋	鬩
xì	戏	戲
xì	饩	餼
xiā	虾	蝦
xiá	辖	轄
xiá	硖	硤
xiá	峡	峽
xiá	侠	俠
xiá	狭	狹
xià	吓	嚇
xiān	鲜	鮮
xiǎn	鲜	鮮
xiān	纤	纖
xiān	跹	躚
xiān	锨	鍁
xiān	莶	薟
xián	贤	賢
xián	咸	鹹

xián	衔	銜
xián	挦	撏
xián	闲	閑
xián	鹇	鷳
xián	娴	嫻
xián	痫	癇
xiǎn	藓	蘚
xiǎn	蚬	蜆
xiǎn	显	顯
xiǎn	险	險
xiǎn	猃	獫
xiǎn	铣	銑
xiàn	献	獻
xiàn	线	綫
xiàn	现	現
xiàn	苋	莧
xiàn	岘	峴
xiàn	县	縣
xiàn	宪	憲
xiàn	馅	餡
xiāng	骧	驤
xiāng	镶	鑲
xiāng	乡	鄉
xiāng	芗	薌
xiāng	缃	緗
xiáng	详	詳
xiǎng	鲞	鮝
xiǎng	响	響
xiǎng	饷	餉
xiǎng	飨	饗
xiàng	向	嚮
xiàng	象	像
xiàng	项	項
xiāo	骁	驍
xiāo	哓	嘵
xiāo	销	銷
xiāo	绡	綃
xiāo	嚣	囂
xiāo	枭	梟
xiāo	鸮	鴞
xiāo	萧	蕭
xiāo	潇	瀟
xiāo	蟏	蠨
xiāo	箫	簫
xiǎo	晓	曉
xiào	啸	嘯
xié	颉	頡
xié	撷	擷
xié	缬	纈
xié	协	協
xié	挟	挾
xié	胁	脅
xié	谐	諧
xiě	写	寫
xiè	亵	褻
xiè	泻	瀉
xiè	绁	紲
xiè	谢	謝
xīn	锌	鋅
xín	寻	尋
xìn	衅	釁
xīng	兴	興
xìng	兴	興
xíng	荥	滎
xíng	钘	鈃
xíng	铏	鉶
xíng	陉	陘
xíng	饧	餳
xiōng	讻	訩
xiòng	诇	詗
xiū	馐	饈
xiū	鸺	鵂
xiù	绣	綉
xiù	锈	銹
xū	顼	頊
xū	须	須
		鬚
xū	谞	諝
xǔ	许	許
xǔ	浒	滸
xǔ	诩	詡
xù	续	續
xù	绪	緒
xuān	轩	軒
xuān	谖	諼
xuán	悬	懸
xuǎn	选	選

Pinyin	Simplified	Traditional
xuǎn	癣	癬
xuàn	旋	鏇
xuàn	铉	鉉
xuàn	绚	絢
xué	学	學
xué	峃	嶨
xuě	鳕	鱈
xuè	谑	謔
xūn	勋	勛
xūn	埙	塤
xún	驯	馴
xún	询	詢
xún	寻	尋
xún	浔	潯
xún	鲟	鱘
xùn	训	訓
xùn	讯	訊
xùn	逊	遜

Y 鸭

Pinyin	Simplified	Traditional
yā	压	壓
yā	鸦	鴉
yā	鸭	鴨
yá	釾	釾
yā	哑	啞
yǎ	哑	啞
yà	氩	氬
yà	亚	亞
yà	垭	埡
yà	挜	掗
yà	娅	婭
yà	讶	訝
yà	轧	軋
yān	阏	閼
yān	阉	閹
yān	恹	懨
yán	颜	顏
yán	盐	鹽
yán	严	嚴
yán	阎	閻
yǎn	厣	厴
yǎn	黡	黶
yǎn	魇	魘
yǎn	俨	儼
yǎn	䶮	龑
yàn	谚	諺
yàn	厌	厭
yàn	餍	饜
yàn	赝	贗
yàn	艳	豔
yàn	滟	灩
yàn	谳	讞
yàn	砚	硯
yàn	觃	覎
yàn	酽	釅
yàn	验	驗
yāng	鸯	鴦
yáng	疡	瘍
yáng	炀	煬
yáng	杨	楊
yáng	扬	揚
yáng	旸	暘
yáng	钖	鍚
yáng	阳	陽
yǎng	痒	癢
yǎng	养	養
yàng	样	樣
yáo	尧	堯
yáo	峣	嶢
yáo	谣	謠
yáo	铫	銚
yáo	轺	軺
yào	疟	瘧
yào	鹞	鷂
yào	钥	鑰
yào	药	藥
yé	爷	爺
yè	靥	靨
yè	页	頁
yè	烨	燁
yè	晔	曄
yè	业	業
yè	邺	鄴
yè	叶	葉
yè	谒	謁

yī	铱	銥	yì	诣	詣	yíng	萦	縈
yī	医	醫	yì	镱	鐿	yíng	营	營
yī	鹥	鷖	yīn	铟	銦	yíng	赢	贏
yī	祎	禕	yīn	阴	陰	yíng	蝇	蠅
yí	颐	頤	yīn	荫	蔭	yǐng	瘿	癭
yí	遗	遺	yìn	荫	蔭	yǐng	颖	穎
yí	仪	儀	yín	龈	齦	yǐng	颖	穎
yí	诒	詒	yín	银	銀	yō	哟	喲
yí	贻	貽	yǐn	饮	飲	yo	哟	喲
yí	饴	飴	yìn	饮	飲	yōng	痈	癰
yǐ	蚁	蟻	yǐn	隐	隱	yōng	拥	擁
yǐ	钇	釔	yǐn	瘾	癮	yōng	佣	傭
yì	谊	誼	yìn	䲟	鮣	yōng	镛	鏞
yì	瘗	瘞	yīng	应	應	yōng	鳙	鱅
yì	镒	鎰	yìng	应	應	yóng	颙	顒
yì	缢	縊	yīng	鹰	鷹	yǒng	踊	踴
yì	勚	勩	yīng	莺	鶯	yōu	忧	憂
yì	怿	懌	yīng	罂	罌	yōu	优	優
yì	译	譯	yīng	婴	嬰	yóu	鱿	魷
yì	驿	驛	yīng	璎	瓔	yóu	犹	猶
yì	峄	嶧	yīng	樱	櫻	yóu	莸	蕕
yì	绎	繹	yīng	撄	攖	yóu	铀	鈾
yì	义	義	yīng	嘤	嚶	yóu	邮	郵
yì	议	議	yīng	鹦	鸚	yǒu	铕	銪
yì	轶	軼	yīng	缨	纓	yòu	诱	誘
yì	艺	藝	yíng	荧	熒	yū	纡	紆
yì	呓	囈	yíng	莹	瑩	yú	舆	輿
yì	亿	億	yíng	茔	塋	yú	欤	歟
yì	忆	憶	yíng	萤	螢	yú	余	餘

yū	觎	覦
yú	谀	諛
yú	鱼	魚
yú	渔	漁
yú	[illegible]	[illegible]
yǔ	与	與
yù	与	與
yǔ	语	語
yù	语	語
yǔ	龉	齬
yǔ	伛	傴
yǔ	屿	嶼
yù	誉	譽
yù	钰	鈺
yù	吁	籲
yù	御	禦
yù	驭	馭
yù	阈	閾
yù	妪	嫗
yù	郁	鬱
yù	谕	諭
yù	鹆	鵒
yù	饫	飫
yù	狱	獄
yù	预	預
yù	滪	澦
yù	蓣	蕷
yù	鹬	鷸
yuān	渊	淵
yuān	鸢	鳶
yuān	鸳	鴛
yuán	鼋	黿
yuán	园	園
yuán	辕	轅
yuán	员	員
yuán	圆	圓
yuán	缘	緣
yuán	橼	櫞
yuǎn	远	遠
yuàn	愿	願
yuē	约	約
yuě	哕	噦
yuè	阅	閱
yuè	钺	鉞
yuè	跃	躍
yuè	乐	樂
yuè	栎	櫟
yuè	钥	鑰
yún	云	雲
yún	芸	蕓
yún	纭	紜
yún	涢	溳
yún	郧	鄖
yǔn	殒	殞
yǔn	陨	隕
yùn	恽	惲
yùn	晕	暈
yūn	晕	暈
yùn	郓	鄆
yùn	运	運
yùn	酝	醞
yùn	韫	韞
yùn	缊	縕
yùn	蕴	蘊

Z
种

zá	杂	雜
za	臜	臢
zǎi	载	載
zài	载	載
zǎn	趱	趲
zǎn	攒	攢
zàn	錾	鏨
zàn	暂	暫
zàn	赞	贊
zàn	瓒	瓚
zāng	赃	贓
zàng	脏	臟
zāng	脏	髒
zǎng	驵	駔
záo	凿	鑿
zǎo	枣	棗
zào	灶	竈
zé	责	責
zé	赜	賾

zē	啧	嘖	zhàn	绽	綻	zhěn	缜	縝
zē	帻	幘	zhàn	颤	顫	zhěn	诊	診
zē	箦	簀	zhàn	栈	棧	zhěn	轸	軫
zē	则	則	zhàn	战	戰	zhèn	鸩	鴆
zē	泽	澤	zhāng	张	張	zhèn	赈	賑
zē	择	擇	zhǎng	长	長	zhèn	镇	鎮
zēi	鲗	鰂	zhǎng	涨	漲	zhèn	纼	紖
zēi	贼	賊	zhàng	涨	漲	zhèn	阵	陣
zèn	谮	譖	zhàng	帐	帳	zhēng	钲	鉦
zēng	缯	繒	zhàng	账	賬	zhèng	钲	鉦
zèng	赠	贈	zhàng	胀	脹	zhēng	征	徵
zèng	锃	鋥	zhāo	钊	釗	zhēng	铮	錚
zhá	铡	鍘	zhào	赵	趙	zhēng	症	癥
zhá	闸	閘	zhào	诏	詔	zhèng	郑	鄭
zhá	轧	軋	zhē	谪	謫	zhèng	证	證
zhǎ	鲝	鮺	zhē	辙	轍	zhèng	帧	幀
zhǎ	鲊	鮓	zhē	蛰	蟄	zhèng	诤	諍
zhà	诈	詐	zhē	辄	輒	zhèng	𬮿	𨴹
zhāi	斋	齋	zhē	詟	讋	zhī	只	隻
zhài	债	債	zhē	折	摺	zhǐ	只	祇
zhān	鹯	鸇	zhě	锗	鍺	zhī	织	織
zhān	鳣	鱣	zhè	这	這	zhí	职	職
zhān	毡	氈	zhè	鹧	鷓	zhí	踯	躑
zhān	觇	覘	zhēn	针	針	zhí	执	執
zhān	谵	譫	zhēn	贞	貞	zhí	絷	縶
zhǎn	斩	斬	zhēn	浈	湞	zhǐ	纸	紙
zhǎn	崭	嶄	zhēn	祯	禎	zhì	挚	摯
zhǎn	盏	盞	zhēn	桢	楨	zhì	贽	贄
zhǎn	辗	輾	zhēn	侦	偵	zhì	鸷	鷙

zhì	掷	擲
zhī	掷	擲
zhì	滞	滯
zhì	栉	櫛
zhì	轾	輊
zhì	致	緻
zhì	帜	幟
zhì	识	識
zhì	制	製
zhì	质	質
zhì	踬	躓
zhì	锧	鑕
zhì	骘	騭
zhōng	终	終
zhōng	钟	鍾
		鐘
zhǒng	种	種
zhòng	种	種
zhǒng	肿	腫
zhòng	众	衆
zhōu	诌	謅
zhōu	赒	賙
zhōu	鸼	鵃
zhóu	轴	軸
zhòu	轴	軸
zhòu	纣	紂
zhòu	荮	葤
zhòu	骤	驟
zhòu	皱	皺
zhòu	绉	縐
zhòu	㤘	㥮
zhòu	㑇	㑳
zhòu	昼	晝
zhū	诸	諸
zhū	槠	櫧
zhū	朱	硃
zhū	诛	誅
zhū	铢	銖
zhú	烛	燭
zhǔ	嘱	囑
zhǔ	瞩	矚
zhù	苎	苧
zhù	贮	貯
zhù	伫	佇
zhù	纻	紵
zhù	驻	駐
zhù	铸	鑄
zhù	筑	築
zhú	筑	築
zhuā	挝	撾
zhuān	专	專
zhuān	砖	磚
zhuān	䏝	膞
zhuān	颛	顓
zhuān	转	轉
zhuǎn	转	轉
zhuàn	啭	囀
zhuàn	赚	賺
zhuàn	传	傳
zhuàn	馔	饌
zhuāng	妆	妝
zhuāng	装	裝
zhuāng	庄	莊
zhuāng	桩	樁
zhuàng	戆	戇
zhuàng	壮	壯
zhuàng	状	狀
zhuī	骓	騅
zhuī	锥	錐
zhuì	赘	贅
zhuì	缒	縋
zhuì	缀	綴
zhuì	坠	墜
zhūn	谆	諄
zhǔn	准	準
zhuō	锗	鐯
zhuó	浊	濁
zhuó	缴	繳
zhuó	诼	諑
zhuó	镯	鐲
zī	谘	諮
zī	资	資
zī	镃	鎡
zī	龇	齜
zī	辎	輜
zī	锱	錙
zī	缁	緇

zī 鲻 鯔		
zì 渍 漬		
zōng 综 綜		
zōng 枞 樅		
zǒng 总 總		
zòng 纵 縱		
zōu 诹 諏		
zōu 鲰 鯫		
zōu 驺 騶		
zōu 邹 鄒		
zú 镞 鏃		
zǔ 诅 詛		
zǔ 组 組		
zuān 钻 鑽		
zuàn 钻 鑽		
zuān 躜 躦		
zuǎn 缵 纘		
zuàn 赚 賺		
zūn 鳟 鱒		
zuò 凿 鑿		

爲 為 为